Australian

Type 2 Diabetes

FOR

DUMMIES®

Australian Edition

Type 2 Diabetes

FOR

DUMMIES®

**Professor Lesley Campbell
and The Diabetes Centre of
St Vincent's Hospital, Sydney
Alan L Rubin, MD**

WILEY

Wiley Publishing Australia Pty Ltd

Type 2 Diabetes For Dummies®, Australian Edition

Published by
Wiley Publishing Australia Pty Ltd
42 McDougall Street
Milton, Qld 4064
www.dummies.com

National Library of Australia
Cataloguing-in-Publication data:

Author:	Campbell, Lesley
Title:	Type 2 Diabetes For Dummies / Lesley Campbell
Edition:	Australian ed
ISBN:	978 1 11830 362 7 (pbk.)
Notes:	Includes index
Subjects:	Non-insulin-dependent diabetes — Treatment — Popular works Diabetes — Diet therapy Patient education
Dewey Number:	616.4624

Cover image: © Akirastock / iStockphoto

Typeset by diacriTech, Chennai, India

Printed in China by
Printplus Limited

10 9 8 7 6 5 4 3 2 1

About the Authors

Professor Lesley Campbell, MBBS FRCP (UK) FRACP AM, is the Director of the Diabetes Centre and Services at St Vincent's Hospital, a Professor of Medicine at the University of NSW, a Senior Researcher at the Garvan Institute of Medical Research and a Senior Physician in clinical practice at St Vincent's Hospital. Her research focuses on type 2 diabetes mellitus and obesity. She's specifically interested in the role of central body fat and the genetic factors predisposing to insulin resistance syndrome and type 2 diabetes.

The **Diabetes Centre** at St Vincent's Hospital in Sydney was established in 1982 to promote greater knowledge about diabetes and optimise its management. The centre is a public specialist health service, staffed by a diabetes specialist, a registrar, diabetes educators and dietitian. It also draws on services including private diabetes specialists, general practitioners, podiatrists, ophthalmologists, psychologists and other health professionals. The aim of the Diabetes Centre's multidisciplinary approach is to help people with diabetes manage their diabetes on a day-to-day basis and facilitate and coordinate the medical, educational and nutritional resources that they need.

Alan L Rubin, MD, is one of America's foremost experts on diabetes. He's a professional member of the American Diabetes Association and the Endocrine Society and has been in private practice specialising in diabetes and thyroid disease for over 25 years.

Authors' Acknowledgements

Acknowledgments from Professor Lesley Campbell

I want to take this opportunity to thank all those who have contributed to this book. My gratitude goes to Melissa Armstrong, who was the main driver in getting this book into production and finally to print. I also want to thank the following people who helped with certain sections of the book: Professor Don Chisholm from the Garvan Institute for Medical Research, Sydney; Dr Jerry Greenfield, Chairman of the Department of Endocrinology at St Vincent's Hospital, Sydney; Dr Paul Lee, Endocrinology Doctoral Candidate from the Garvan Insitute for Medical Research; Jane Ludington, Clinical Pharmacist from St Vincent's Hospital and the University of Sydney; Dr Louise Maple-Brown from the Menzies School of Health Research in Darwin; Dr Gabrielle O'Kane, Microbiologist/Registrar in Diabetes at St Vincent's Hospital; Dr Ann Poynton, Endocrinologist from Prince of Wales Hospital, Sydney; Dr Vanessa Tsang from Royal North Shore Hospital, Sydney; Dr Daniel Chen, Registrar in Endocrinology at St Vincent's Hospital; Dr Kay Wilhelm and Joanna Crawford from the Urban Mental Health Research Institute St Vincent's Hospital; Dr Weng Sam, Visiting Medical Officer, Department of Endocrinology at St Vincent's Hospital; and Karen Jameson, Diabetes Educator at Royal North Shore Hospital in Sydney.

This book wouldn't have been possible without the help of the staff at the Diabetes Centre at St Vincent's Hospital in Sydney. I again thank Melissa Armstrong and also Kylie Alexander, Jan Alford, Wendy Bryant, Cathy Carty, Josie Maguire and Penny Morris.

Acknowledgments from Doctor Alan Rubin

I want to thank ophthalmologist Dr John Norris of Pacific Eye Associates in San Francisco for helping me to see the place of the eye physician in diabetes care. I also want to thank podiatrist Dr Mark Pinter for helping me get a leg-up on his specialty. Librarians Mary Ann Zaremska and Nancy Phelps at St Francis Memorial Hospital were tremendously helpful in providing the articles and books upon which the information in the book is based.

My teachers are too numerous to mention, but one group deserves special attention. They are my patients over the last 26 years, the people whose trials and tribulations caused me to seek the knowledge that you find in this book.

Dedication

We dedicate this book to the people with diabetes we've met over the years who have taught us so much and from whom we are still learning — Prof Lesley Campbell and the St Vincent's Hospital Diabetes Team.

This book is dedicated to my wife, Enid, and my children, Renee and Larry. Their patience, enthusiasm, and encouragement helped to make the writing a real pleasure — Alan L Rubin.

Publisher's Acknowledgements

We're proud of this book; please send us your comments through our online registration form located at http://dummies.custhelp.com.

Some of the people who helped bring this book to market include the following:

Acquisitions, Editorial and Media Development

Project Editors: Dani Karvess, Elizabeth Whiley

Acquisitions Editor: Rebecca Crisp

Editorial Manager: Hannah Bennett

Production

Cartoons: Glenn Lumsden

Proofreader: Charlotte Duff

Indexer: Don Jordan, Antipodes Indexing

Every effort has been made to trace the ownership of copyright material. Information that enables the publisher to rectify any error or omission in subsequent editions is welcome. In such cases, please contact the Permissions Section of John Wiley & Sons Australia, Ltd.

Contents at a Glance

Table of Contents

Introduction

● ●

*Y*ou may be thinking nothing is lucky about being diagnosed with type 2 diabetes; after all, it's a disease, isn't it? And you're right, nothing is lucky about the diagnosis, but the people who are diagnosed with diabetes early on in the 21st century are the luckiest group in history.

Those of you with diabetes have a decade or more in which to avoid the long-term complications of this disease. In a sense, a diagnosis of diabetes is both good news and bad news. It's bad news because you have a disease you would happily do without. It's good news if you use it to make some changes in your lifestyle that can not only prevent complications but also help you to live a longer and higher quality of life.

As for developing a sense of humour about it, at times you'll feel like doing anything but laughing. But scientific studies are clear about the benefits of a positive attitude. In a very few words: He who laughs, lasts. Another point is that people learn more and retain more when humour is part of the process.

Our goal isn't to trivialise human suffering by being comic about it, but to lighten the burden of a chronic disease by showing that it's not all gloom and doom.

About This Book

The book isn't meant to be read from cover to cover — although if you know nothing about diabetes, doing so might be a good approach. This book is your source of information on diabetes and the medical research under way at the time of writing into new drugs and techniques. So that you may stay abreast of the latest developments in diabetes care, the book also directs you to the best sources of reliable information on any medical advances that may occur after the publication of this edition.

We only cover type 2 diabetes in this book. If you're curious about other types of diabetes, including type 1 and gestational diabetes, *Diabetes For Dummies, 3rd Australian Edition* (published by Wiley Publishing Australia Pty Ltd), is a good resource for you.

We've tried to provide you with enough information so that you can make informed decisions about how you can care for yourself when you have type 2 diabetes, but always remember that you have your GP and members of your diabetes care team to help you through. You're not alone!

Conventions Used in this Book

Diabetes, as you know, is all about sugar. But sugars come in many types. So health professionals avoid using the words sugar and glucose interchangeably. In this book (unless we slip up), we use the word glucose rather than sugar.

What You Don't Have to Read

Throughout the book, shaded areas, called sidebars, appear. These sidebars contain material that's interesting but not essential. We hereby give you permission to skip them if the material inside them is of no particular interest to you.

Foolish Assumptions

This book assumes that you know nothing about diabetes. You won't suddenly have to face a term that's not explained and that you've never heard of before. For those of you who already know a lot, we provide more in-depth explanations. You can pick and choose how much you want to know about a subject, but the key points are clearly marked.

How This Book Is Organised

This book is divided into four parts to help you to find out all you can about the topic of type 2 diabetes.

Part I: Dealing with the Onset of Type 2 Diabetes

To slay the dragon, you have to be able to identify it. This part explains type 2 diabetes and how you get it, as well as some advice on how to deal with the emotional and psychological consequences of the diagnosis and what all those big words mean. We've also included details on ways to prevent progressing to type 2 diabetes to inform you, among other things, about the latest advances in research in this area.

Part II: How Type 2 Diabetes Affects Your Body

Few diseases affect every part of the body in the way that diabetes does. If you understand diabetes, you'll have a fairly good grasp of how other illnesses can change the state of your health.

In this part, you find out what you need to know about both the short- and long-term complications of diabetes.

Part III: Living with Type 2 Diabetes: Your Physical Health

In this part, you discover all the tools available to treat diabetes. You find out about the kinds of tests that you should be doing as well as the tests your doctor should be ordering to get a clear picture of your diabetes, what to do about it and how to follow treatment. We've also provided information about medications that can help to control your diabetes.

We make lots of recommendations for dietary changes that can help control your blood glucose and detail how to get the most out of your exercise routine.

Part IV: The Part of Tens

This part presents some key suggestions — the things you most need to know as well as the things you least want to know. You discover the ten commandments of diabetes care and the myths that confuse many people who have diabetes.

Icons Used in This Book

The icons tell you what you must know, what you should know and what you might find interesting but can live without.

This icon marks whenever we tell a story about people with diabetes.

Pay attention when you see this icon; it means the information is essential and you need to be aware of it.

This icon points out when you should see your doctor or a member of your diabetes care team (for example, if your blood glucose level is too high or you need a particular test done).

The information provided here is more complex, so you can skip it if you choose.

Listen up. This icon marks important information that can save you time and energy.

When you see this icon, take note. It warns against potential problems (for example, if you don't treat something).

Part I

Dealing with the Onset of Type 2 Diabetes

Glenn Lumsden

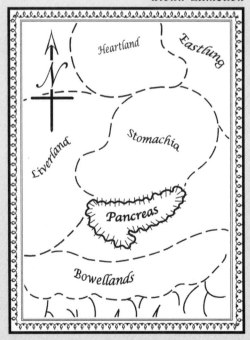

'Pancreas: A small region, often ignored, until it goes on strike.'

In this part ...

*Y*ou've been told that you or a loved one has type 2
diabetes. What do you do now? This part helps you
to deal with all the emotions that inevitably arise — from
wondering whether the diagnosis is correct to investigating
the causes of type 2 diabetes.

Chapter 1

Dealing with Type 2 Diabetes

- -

In This Chapter

▶ Developing techniques to live with diabetes

▶ Getting used to the idea of having diabetes

▶ Looking at why your mental health is important

▶ Maintaining a high quality of life after diagnosis

- -

*I*f you've picked up this book, chances are you or someone you know has been diagnosed with type 2 diabetes. A diagnosis of any medical condition is simply a way of understanding that condition by putting it in a category that helps to predict what's likely to happen to you. A diagnosis also allows doctors and health care professionals to make assumptions about your treatment and prognosis. A diagnosis is, where possible, based on evidence.

However, if you have diabetes, you're more than a diagnosis or a measurement of abnormal blood glucose levels. You have feelings and a history. The way that you respond to the challenges of diabetes helps to determine whether the disease is a moderate annoyance or a source of major sickness.

You're not alone. Type 2 diabetes is a common disease, and getting more common. *Diabetes shouldn't stop you from doing what you want to do with your life.* We encourage you to follow the guidelines of good diabetes care, which we describe in Part III. If you follow the guidelines, you can often be just as healthy as the person without diabetes.

Also, your diabetes doesn't affect just one person. Your family, friends and colleagues are affected by how you deal with your diabetes and by their desire to help you. In this chapter, we introduce you to what it means to be diagnosed with type 2 diabetes, the kinds of feelings you may struggle with after diagnosis and how you can move forward and learn to live with diabetes.

Living with Type 2 Diabetes

Diabetes is a chronic disease that can create short- and long-term complications (see Chapters 4 and 5 for more). Here are some tips for living with type 2 diabetes:

- **Get to know the doctors, nurses and other health professionals involved in your care.** Identify people you feel comfortable with and agree with on what works for you. You want to share a common vision and treatment plan with your doctor and treating team. Ensure you have a general practitioner you can relate to and stick with one rather than choosing to just turn up at a medical centre.

- **Keep a list of questions.** Have a list of questions for your doctor or diabetes care team. Write these down when you think of them and take them with you on your next visit.

- **Find out if you can talk to people who have managed their diabetes well.** Most people know someone with diabetes, but that doesn't mean they know what's best for you to do, or anything about your diabetes. Your diabetes care team, the Australian Diabetes Council (in NSW) or Diabetes Australia (in other states and territories) can help you get in touch with people whose circumstances are (or were) similar to yours. You may also know someone within your circle of family, friends or colleagues.

- **Surround yourself with loving positive support.** With luck, you not only accept the diabetes diagnosis yourself, but you also share the news with your family, friends and people close to you. Having diabetes isn't something to be ashamed of and isn't something that you should hide from anyone. Identify who's 'there for you' and let those people know you appreciate it. If possible, give them things they can do — people do better when they have a tangible way of supporting you.

✔ **Understand how you cope with stressful situations and change, and build healthy coping skills.** Diabetes often starts at times of stress — just when you don't need another thing to be happening. Being diagnosed with the condition presents you with an opportunity to reflect on how you deal with stress and what kind of coping skills you have developed. When it comes to your long-term health — both physical and mental — adopting coping skills that are healthy and help you build and maintain your motivation for making lifestyle changes pays off.

✔ **Make sure you have good information.** Reading this book is a great start! Your next step is to find out about other reliable sources of information and support. Excellent resources are available and your diabetes care team is available to assist. Throughout the book, we provide details of useful websites for further information about diabetes. Here are some to get you started:

- **Australian Diabetes Council:** Previously known as Diabetes Australia NSW. Provides information about all aspects of diabetes. www.australiandiabetescouncil.com.au

- **Australian Diabetes Educators Association:** This is the official website of the organisation representing diabetes educators in Australia. www.adea.com.au

- **Baker IDI Heart and Diabetes Institute:** This Victorian-based institute is the largest diabetes clinic in Australia. www.bakeridi.edu.au

- **Diabetes Australia:** Diabetes Australia has branches in all states and territories except NSW. They represent people with diabetes, research organisations, doctors and other health professionals involved with diabetes. www.diabetesaustralia.com.au

Adjusting to the Diagnosis

Getting used to a diagnosis of diabetes can take some adjustment. You may also feel an unjust stigma is attached to type 2 diabetes. You may feel that some people think it's your fault that you developed diabetes — that it was caused simply by eating too much and not exercising enough.

As well as having to deal with the stigma attached to having type 2 diabetes, you may also have to deal with guilt. Type 2 diabetes may occur, for some, after they feel they have neglected their health. In this case, some people 'beat themselves up' after being diagnosed. While this is understandable, like anger, it's unnecessary and destructive. Think about what you can learn from your diagnosis and what steps you can take to improve your health. See Chapters 8 and 9 for more on improving your health through making changes to your diet and exercise.

A diagnosis of type 2 diabetes may also occur in people who take certain medications (such as prednisone or olanzapine) long term. Again, developing diabetes in this case isn't your fault and the medications may be something you need to continue. Talk to your doctor and diabetes care team about what medications you should be taking (and should continue to take) to ensure full physical health. See Chapter 7 for more on medications.

Having type 2 diabetes can also affect, or be affected by, other aspects of your life. If you are overweight or unfit, talk to your GP or specialist diabetes dietitian about developing an eating and exercise plan to improve your overall health. Some people can improve the control of their type 2 diabetes by improving their general fitness, while some can't. Even if you still require medication to manage your diabetes, it's still worth incorporating more exercise into your daily routine, because improving fitness helps improve your general physical and mental health.

If you have previous mental health problems, talk them over with your GP, psychologist or counsellor. If you've had episodes of depression, anxiety, eating disorders, substance abuse (alcohol, sedatives and street drugs), these can recur when you are stressed and affect your diabetes.

Working On Your Mental Health

Mental health is now recognised as a key issue in the management of diabetes. People with diagnosed diabetes are twice as likely to experience depression or anxiety compared with people without diabetes. People newly diagnosed often also have to move through feelings of anger. The following sections look at these common and understandable reactions, as well as offering information on where to go for more help if your feelings of anger and depression become more long lasting.

Dealing with depression

Experts now recognise a two-way relationship exists between diabetes, stress and depression. Stress can precipitate the onset of diabetes, and ongoing diabetes-related distress has a direct effect on blood sugar levels. In turn, the pressure of living with a chronic disease can affect your mental health and capacity to cope with daily life.

Depression can make it more difficult for you to self-manage your diabetes. Depression can decrease concentration and motivation, and affect lifestyle and exercise habits, as well as pain tolerance and overall mood — which in turn affects your diabetes. If depression isn't treated in people with diabetes, it can affect blood sugar levels and contribute to more diabetes-related complications.

The good news is that this cycle can be reversed. By taking steps to use more helpful ways of coping with diabetes and by treating mental illness, you can improve your mental health, increase your confidence in managing your diabetes and increase your motivation for self-care and making required lifestyle changes, such as adopting healthy eating patterns (see Chapter 8) and increasing physical activity (see Chapter 9). These changes, in turn, can improve your physical health.

Getting through your anger

Anger often keeps you from successfully managing your diabetes — as long as you're angry, you're not in a problem-solving mode. Diabetes requires your focus and attention. Turn your anger into creative ways to manage your diabetes. (For ways to manage your diabetes, see Part III.)

Don't be discouraged if you're irritable, angry, guilty, anxious or miserable for a short time. These are natural coping mechanisms that serve a psychological purpose for a brief time. Allow yourself to have these feelings — and then drop them. You then need to move on and learn to live normally with your diabetes.

When you're having trouble coping

You wouldn't hesitate to seek help for your physical ailments associated with diabetes, but you may be very reluctant to seek help when you can't adjust psychologically to diabetes. The problem is that, sooner or later, your psychological problems can affect the control that you have over your diabetes. And, of course, you won't lead a very pleasant life if you're in a depressed or anxious state all the time. Symptoms to indicate that you may be suffering from depression include insomnia, fatigue, lack of appetite, not being able to think clearly, feeling worthless or having frequent thoughts of suicide, and finding no humour or amusement in anything.

If you recognise several of these symptoms as features of your daily life, you need to get some help. Your sense of hopelessness may include the feeling that no-one else can help you — and that simply isn't true. Your GP, psychologist and/or endocrinologist are the people to go to for advice. They can help you to find the best treatment for your psychological difficulties.

Well-trained counsellors whom you trust — especially counsellors who are trained to take care of people with diabetes — can help you find solutions that you can't envisage in your current state. Taking part in a support group might also help.

Your doctor may decide that your situation requires medication to help treat the anxiety or depression. At the time of writing, many drugs are available that are proven to be safe and relatively free of side effects. Sometimes a brief period of medication is enough to help you adjust to your diabetes.

More coping styles and psychological therapies are discussed in *Diabetes For Dummies, 3rd Australian Edition.*

The Way Forward After Diagnosis

You may assume that a chronic condition like diabetes leads to a diminished quality of life for you. But must this be the case? What can you do to maintain a high quality of life with diabetes? Here are the steps that accomplish the most for you:

✔ Keep your blood glucose levels as close to normal as possible (see Part III).

✔ Make exercise a regular part of your lifestyle.

✔ Get plenty of support from family, friends, and medical resources.

✔ Stay abreast of the latest developments in diabetes care.

✔ Maintain a healthy attitude.

Learning healthy ways of coping with diabetes and how to manage stress or depression can also help you cope with other challenges and improve your overall quality of life.

Chapter 2

It's the Glucose

*T*he Greeks and Romans knew about diabetes. Fortunately, the way they tested for the condition — by tasting people's urine — has gone by the wayside. In this way, the Romans discovered that the urine of certain people was *mellitus*, the Latin word for *sweet*. The Greeks noticed that when people with sweet urine drank, the fluids came out in the urine almost as fast as they went in the mouth, like a siphon. They called this by the Greek word for *siphon* — *diabetes*. This is the origin of the modern name for the disease, diabetes mellitus.

In this chapter, we cover the not-so-fun stuff about diabetes — the big words, the definitions and so on. But if you really want to understand what's happening to your body when you have diabetes, you won't want to skip this chapter, despite the technical words.

Recognising Diabetes

The sweetness of the urine comes from *glucose*, also known as blood sugar. Many different kinds of sugars occur naturally, but glucose is the sugar that has the starring role in the body, providing a source of instant energy so that muscles can move and important chemical reactions can take place. Sugar is a carbohydrate, one group of the three sources of energy in the body. The others are protein and fat, which we discuss in greater detail in Chapter 8.

Table sugar, or *sucrose*, is actually two different kinds of sugar — glucose and fructose — linked together. Fructose is the type of sugar found in fruits and vegetables. It's sweeter than glucose, which makes sucrose sweeter than glucose as well. Your taste buds require less sucrose or fructose to get the same sweetening power of glucose.

In order to understand the symptoms of diabetes, you need to know a little about the way the body normally handles glucose and what happens when things go wrong. The following sections cover detecting diabetes and the fine line that your body treads between control and lack of control of its glucose levels.

Testing for diabetes

The standard definition of diabetes mellitus is excessive glucose in a blood sample. The Australian standard for diagnosis endorsed by the Royal Australian College of General Practitioners (RACGP) and Diabetes Australia requires that the diagnosis of diabetes is made by using any one of the following three criteria:

- *Random plasma glucose* concentration greater than or equal to 11.1 mmol/L along with symptoms of diabetes (see the section 'Losing control of glucose' later in this chapter). The abbreviation *mmol/L* stands for *millimoles per litre*. Other countries may use the units *mg/dl*, which is *milligrams per decilitre*. To get mg/dl, you multiply mmol/L by 18.

- *Fasting plasma glucose (FPG)* of greater than or equal to 7 mmol/L. *Fasting* means that the patient has consumed no food for eight hours prior to the test.

- *Blood glucose* of greater than or equal to 11.1 mmol/L, when tested two hours (2-h PG) after ingesting 75 grams of glucose by mouth (carried out after an overnight fast following three days of adequate carbohydrate intake of greater than 200 grams per day). This test has long been known as the *oral glucose tolerance test* (OGTT). Although this test is rarely done because it takes time and is cumbersome, it remains the gold standard for the diagnosis of diabetes and should be carried out in a patient with a borderline result. This test isn't necessary in patients whose random plasma glucose level is greater or equal to 11.1 mmol/L, or whose fasting plasma glucose is greater or equal to 7 mmol/L.

If a fasting plasma glucose is between 5.5 and 7.0 mmol/L or a random plasma glucose concentration is between 7.8 mmol/L and 11.1 mmol/L on two separate occasions, an OGTT should be carried out to support or exclude a diagnosis of diabetes. If a fasting plasma glucose concentration is greater than 7 mmol/L on two separate occasions, this confirms a diagnosis of diabetes. If an OGTT is greater than 11.1 mmol/L, this confirms a diagnosis of diabetes.

Putting it another way:

- ✔ FPG less than 5.5 mmol/L is a normal fasting glucose.

- ✔ FPG greater than or equal to 6 mmol/L but less than 7.0 mmol/L is impaired fasting glucose (indicating prediabetes — see Chapter 3 for information about prediabetes).

- ✔ FPG equal to or greater than 7.0 mmol/L gives a provisional diagnosis of diabetes.

During an OGTT:

- ✔ 2-h PG less than 7.8 mmol/L is normal glucose tolerance.

- ✔ 2-h PG greater than or equal to 7.8 mmol/L but less than 11.1 mmol/L is impaired glucose tolerance, which indicates disordered carbohydrate metabolism, which can lead to diabetes.

- ✔ 2-h PG equal to or greater than 11.1 mmol/L gives a diagnosis of diabetes.

Controlling glucose

A hormone called *insulin* finely controls the level of glucose in your blood. A *hormone* is a chemical substance made in one part of the body that travels (usually through the bloodstream) to a distant part of the body where it performs its work. In the case of insulin, that work is to act like a key to open the inside of a cell, such as muscle, fat or other cells, so that glucose can enter. If glucose can't enter the cell, it can provide no energy to the body.

Insulin is essential for growth. In addition to providing the key to entry of glucose into the cell, scientists consider insulin the builder hormone. It enables fat and muscle to form. It promotes storage of glucose in a form called glycogen for use when fuel isn't coming in. It blocks breakdown of protein. Without insulin, you don't survive for long. (See the section 'Getting to Know Your Pancreas' later in this chapter for more information about insulin.)

With this finetuning, the body manages to keep the level of glucose fairly steady at about 3.3 to 6.4 mmol/L all the time.

Losing control of glucose

Your glucose starts to rise in your blood when insulin is either not present in sufficient quantity or isn't working effectively. Once your glucose rises above 10.0 mmol/L, glucose begins to spill into the urine and make it sweet. Up to that point, the kidney, the filter for the blood, is able to extract the glucose before it enters your urine. It's the loss of glucose into the urine that leads to many of the short-term complications of diabetes. (See Chapter 4 for information on short-term complications.)

The following list notes the most common early symptoms of diabetes and how they occur. One or more of the following symptoms may be present when diabetes is diagnosed:

- ✔ **Frequent urination and thirst:** The glucose in the urine draws more water out of the blood, so more urine forms. More urine in your bladder makes you feel the need to urinate more frequently during the day and to get up at night to empty the bladder, which keeps filling up. As the amount of water in your blood declines, you feel thirsty and drink much more frequently.

- ✔ **Fatigue:** Because glucose can't enter cells that depend on insulin as a key for glucose (the most important exception is the brain, which doesn't need insulin), glucose can't be used as a fuel to move muscles or to facilitate the many other chemical reactions that have to take place to produce energy. The person with diabetes often complains of fatigue and feels much stronger once treatment allows glucose to enter cells again.

- ✔ **Weight loss:** Weight loss is common among some people with diabetes because they lack insulin, which is the builder hormone. When insulin is lacking for any reason, the body begins to break down and you lose muscle tissue. Some of the muscle converts into glucose even though it can't get into cells. It passes out of your body in the urine. Fat tissue breaks down into small fat particles that can provide an alternative source of energy. As your body breaks down and you lose glucose in the urine, you often experience weight loss. However, most people with diabetes are heavy rather than skinny.

✓ **Persistent vaginal infection among women:** As blood glucose rises, all the fluids in your body contain higher levels of glucose, including sweat and body secretions such as semen in men and vaginal secretions in women. Many bugs, such as bacteria and fungi, thrive in the high-glucose environment. Women begin to complain of itching or burning, an abnormal discharge from the vagina, and sometimes an odour.

Getting to Know Your Pancreas

The pancreas has two major functions. One is to produce *digestive enzymes*, which are the chemicals in your small intestine that help to break down the food that you eat. The digestive enzymes don't have much relation to diabetes, so we won't focus on them in this book. Your pancreas's other function is to produce and secrete directly into the blood a hormone of major importance: *Insulin.*

Figure 2-1 shows the cellular make-up of the pancreas. The cells that are relevant to diabetes are the beta cells, which create the key hormone, insulin, and the alpha cells, which produce glucagon, a hormone that raises glucose levels. The insulin-producing pancreas cells are found in groups called *Islets of Langerhans.*

If you understand only one hormone in your body, insulin should be that hormone (especially if you want to understand diabetes). Over the course of your life, the insulin that your body produces or the insulin that you inject into your body (see Chapter 7) affects whether or not you control your diabetes and avoid the complications of the disease.

Think of your insulin as an insurance agent who lives in Sydney (which is your pancreas) but travels from there to do business in Melbourne (your muscles), Brisbane (your fat tissue), Adelaide (your liver), and other places. This insulin insurance agent is insuring your good health.

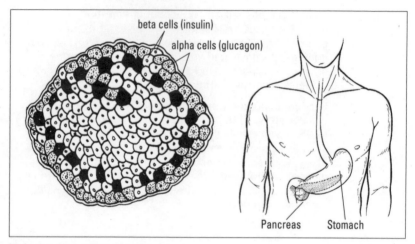

Figure 2-1: The pancreas and its parts.

Wherever insulin travels in your body, it opens up the cells so that glucose can enter them. After it enters them, the cells can immediately use glucose for energy, store it in a storage form of glucose (called *glycogen*) for rapid use later on, or convert it to fat for use even later as energy. After glucose leaves your blood and enters your cells, your blood glucose level falls. Your pancreas can detect when your glucose level is falling, and it turns off the release of insulin to prevent unhealthy low levels of blood glucose called *hypoglycaemia* from developing (see Chapter 4). At the same time, your liver begins to release glucose from storage and makes new glucose from amino acids in your blood.

If your insurance agent (insulin) does a poor job when he does show up (such as when you have a resistance to insulin, as in type 2 diabetes), your insurance coverage may be very poor (in which case, your blood glucose starts to climb). High blood glucose is where all your problems begin. Medical research has proved conclusively that high blood glucose is bad for the body, and that keeping the levels of blood glucose as normal as possible prevents the complications of diabetes (see Part II). Most treatments for diabetes are directed at restoring the blood glucose to normal.

Discovering Ways to Treat Diabetes

A condition that must have been diabetes mellitus appeared in the writings of China and India more than 2,000 years ago but it wasn't until 1776 that researchers discovered the cause — glucose. And it wasn't until the 19th century that doctors developed a new chemical test. Later discoveries showed that the pancreas produces a crucial substance, called insulin, that controls the glucose in the blood. Since that time, insulin has been extracted and purified enough to save many lives. Oral drugs to reduce blood glucose became available only in the last 40 years.

Once insulin was discovered, diabetes specialists, led by Elliot Joslin and others, recommended three basic treatments for diabetes that are as valuable today as they were in 1921: Diet (see Chapter 8), exercise (see Chapter 9) and medication (see Chapter 7).

The next major discovery was the group of drugs called *sulphonylureas* (see Chapter 7), the first drugs that could be taken by mouth to lower the blood glucose. But the only way to know the level of the blood glucose was still by testing the urine, which was entirely inadequate for good control of diabetes (see Chapter 6).

Around 1980, the first portable meters for blood glucose testing became available. For the first time, it was possible to relate treatment to a measurable outcome. This has led, in turn, to the discovery of other great drugs for diabetes, such as acarbose, thiazolidinediones, DPP-IV inhibitors and exanitide.

If you're not using these wonderful tools for your diabetes, you're missing the boat. You can find out exactly how to use them in Part III.

Telling a Typical Patient Story

The statistics on diagnosed cases of diabetes don't begin to reflect the human dimensions of the disease. People finally take the appropriate tests after days or months (or even years) of minor discomforts that reach the point where they can no longer be tolerated. The following story of an actual patient can help you understand that diabetes is a disease that can strike people at any time. (Please note that we've changed the patient's name.)

Terry Lee was a 46-year-old black-belt taekwondo instructor. Despite his active lifestyle, he wasn't careful about his diet and had gained seven kilograms in the last few years. He was more fatigued than he'd been in the past but blamed this on his increasing age. His mother had diabetes, but he assumed that his physical fitness would protect him from this condition. He was finding that he could barely get through a one-hour class without needing a toilet break. The symptoms of fatigue and frequent urination got worse, and he finally made an appointment with his GP. Blood tests revealed a random blood glucose of 14.7 mmol/L. The following week, a fasting blood glucose was done through the laboratory — with a result of 11.2 mmol/L. The doctor told Terry he had diabetes, but Terry refused to believe it. He left the doctor's office in an angry mood but vowed to lose weight and did so successfully. On a repeat visit to the doctor, a random glucose was 9.3 mmol/L. However, his symptoms continued. He finally returned to the doctor and was found to have a random blood glucose of 16.8 mmol/L. Finally, he accepted the diagnosis and started treatment. He rapidly returned to his usual state of health, and the fatigue disappeared. He was a bit cross with himself for being so stubborn!

Chapter 3

Understanding the Transition to Type 2 Diabetes

Type 2 diabetes is becoming a worldwide 'epidemic'. At the time of writing, approximately 285 million people have type 2 diabetes, and numbers are predicted to reach 438 million by 2030. At least 50 per cent of those with type 2 diabetes remain undiagnosed. In Australia, one in four adults has a disturbance in how glucose is metabolised in the body.

Levels of obesity in Australia are increasing while the amount of physical activity we do is declining. Obesity and physical inactivity are two significant lifestyle risk factors for developing type 2 diabetes. Although genetics contribute strongly to both the rise in obesity and the rise in diabetes, the escalation of these conditions appears to be due to an imbalance between energy intake and the expenditure of energy through physical exertion and activity.

We provide information in this chapter to help you identify whether you're at risk of *prediabetes* (a mildly increased level of glucose in your blood) and how you can manage it. We also explain the causes of type 2 diabetes and how you can avoid progressing towards it. Lastly, we cover what happens if you are diagnosed with type 2 diabetes.

Knowing What Puts You at Risk of Prediabetes

The risk factors for developing prediabetes are the same as the risk factors for developing type 2 diabetes. Genetic inheritance causes type 2 diabetes. However, lifestyle factors such as obesity and lack of exercise interact with genetic risk to trigger the disease. People with type 2 diabetes are insulin-resistant before they become obese or sedentary. Subsequently, ageing, poor eating habits, obesity and failure to exercise combine to bring out the disease.

High-risk groups for type 2 diabetes include people who

- ✔ Are over the age of 55

- ✔ Have cardiovascular disease

- ✔ Have a history of gestational diabetes

- ✔ Are overweight (and especially those with increased waist measurements)

- ✔ Smoke

- ✔ Have high blood pressure (hypertension)

- ✔ Have a family history of type 2 diabetes

- ✔ Are from indigenous populations

- ✔ Are from high-risk ethnic groups, such as South-East Asians, Indians and Pacific Islanders

- ✔ Have polycystic ovary disease (a common condition in women who have an over-secretion of insulin)

Identifying those individuals who are most at risk is vital. Anyone who displays the signs and symptoms of diabetes should consult a doctor immediately.

Obviously, you can't do anything about some of these risk factors — like who your parents are — but you can modify other factors (see the section 'Turning Back the Clock').

Populations at risk

A number of early warning signs appear in populations that are most at risk of developing type 2 diabetes. In developing countries, where often people don't have enough food, those whose genetic makeup enables their bodies to use carbohydrates in a very efficient manner have an advantage over the rest of the population because they can survive on a low intake of food and kilojoules. Perhaps when they were young, these people didn't make enough insulin-producing cells because they didn't need them for their reduced food intake. If these people receive ample supplies of food, their bodies are overwhelmed. Their pancreases may not have enough insulin-producing cells to handle the load and they're likely to become fat and sedentary and develop diabetes. This may explain why people in developing countries are the most at risk of developing type 2 diabetes. Population studies show that the incidence of diabetes is greatest in developing countries such as China and India.

Apart from a family history of diabetes, an illness of any sort, and particularly an infection, can increase the risk of prediabetes. Some medications (especially cortisone-related drugs and some medications used to treat severe mental illness) can also increase your risk of developing prediabetes (or diabetes). Ask your GP if any of your prescribed medications could increase your blood glucose levels and, if they do, get your GP to test your fasting glucose level regularly. You may not be able to stop these medications, so it's important to be screened at least once a year for diabetes so a diagnosis can be picked up as soon as possible after it occurs.

Be on the lookout for any signs of very high blood glucose levels, such as excessive thirst and increased urination, fatigue or poor healing, which could indicate your condition has progressed to diabetes. (See the section 'Discovering You Have Type 2 Diabetes' for a detailed list of the symptoms.)

Always see your doctor if you experience any of these symptoms for longer than a week or so.

Diagnosising Prediabetes

After submitting a sample of your blood for testing, your GP may tell you the sample showed a mild increase in your blood glucose levels, explaining these levels were outside the normal range but not high enough to diagnose type 2 diabetes. These mild increases have been given the name *prediabetes* and indicate an increased risk of developing type 2 diabetes, and also of developing cardiovascular disease.

In the next sections, we discuss how prediabetes is diagnosed (through glucose testing). We also discuss what happens when you get given a diagnosis of prediabetes.

Testing for prediabetes

Prediabetes is often described as either impaired fasting glucose (IFG) or impaired glucose tolerance (IGT). These conditions are slightly different, but both diagnoses indicate that without some intervention your chance of progressing to type 2 diabetes is much higher.

Impaired fasting glucose

The diagnosis of impaired fasting glucose (IFG) can be made based on a simple blood test from your doctor. This test should be done after an overnight fast — in other words, no food or drink after midnight on the previous evening.

A fasting plasma glucose reading of 6.1 to 6.9 mmol/L means that you have impaired fasting glucose. Levels of 7 or above indicate a diagnosis of diabetes — in this case, you've already gone past the 'pre' part. The diabetes experts from the American Diabetes Association suggest that the diagnosis of IFG should be made from levels of 5.6 mmol/L upwards, but this hasn't yet been accepted internationally.

For this reason, if you have a blood test reading in the 'we're not sure' range — that is, between 5.6 and 6.9 mmol/L — the recommendation from the Australian Diabetes Society is that you should have an oral glucose tolerance test (OGTT) to determine whether or not you have diabetes, IFG or impaired glucose tolerance (see following section).

After the OGTT, your doctor diagnoses you with IFG if your blood samples show the following:

- ✔ Your fasting plasma glucose reading is between 6.1 and 6.9 mmol/L
- ✔ Your follow-up two-hour level is less than 7.8 mmol/L

An important difference between IFG and impaired glucose tolerance (IGT) is that with IFG your blood glucose levels don't rise abnormally two hours after you've taken the sweet drink, while with IGT they do. IFG is more common in men.

Impaired glucose tolerance

A diagnosis of impaired glucose tolerance (IGT), which is more common in women, is made on the basis of the OGTT described in the preceding section.

After the OGTT, your doctor diagnoses you with IGT if your blood samples show the following:

- ✔ Your fasting plasma glucose is less than 7 mmol/L
- ✔ Your follow-up two-hour level is between 7.8 and 11.0 mmol/L

If your fasting level in the OGTT is above 7 or your follow-up two-hour level is above 11 mmol/L, you go straight to being diagnosed with diabetes.

Deciphering the diagnosis

Being diagnosed with either IFG or IGT (refer to the preceding section) indicates that you have a greatly increased chance of developing type 2 diabetes; hence the term 'prediabetes'. Various studies have shown that, each year, 3 to 11 per cent of people with prediabetes develop diabetes. The good news is that progression to diabetes isn't inevitable. When followed up some years later, approximately one-third of people with prediabetes had progressed to diabetes, one-third had remained the same and one-third had returned to normal glucose tolerance.

However, don't relax yet! Apart from the increased risk of developing diabetes, the diagnosis of prediabetes also indicates a substantially increased risk of cardiovascular disease (including problems such as heart attack and stroke).

This relationship between abnormal blood glucose levels and cardiovascular risk is strongly associated with abdominal obesity — that is, carrying excess weight around your middle area — and has been termed 'the metabolic syndrome' (see Chapter 5).

Although the increased risk of cardiovascular problems isn't as great as in established diabetes, it's still significant — approximately twice the risk of someone without prediabetes. Therefore, you should be checked out by your GP for all the cardiovascular risk factors.

The following lists what your GP should check to monitor both your diabetes and cardiovascular wellbeing, and when:

- ✔ Blood pressure — at every visit to your GP

- ✔ Cholesterol and other blood fats — once a year

- ✔ Weight — at every visit

Perhaps not surprisingly, the lifestyle changes you can make to reduce your cardiovascular risk factors are the same as those that reduce your risk of progressing to diabetes. These include improving the quality of your diet, increasing your physical activity and quitting smoking (see the following section for more).

If you're diagnosed with prediabetes, you need to monitor your blood glucose levels, but don't worry — you don't have to start using finger-prick blood glucose testing just yet (see Chapter 6 for more on this monitoring method). You need to do a blood test to check your fasting blood glucose level once a year, so your GP can determine whether you've progressed to type 2 diabetes and work out if further action is necessary.

Turning Back the Clock

Not everyone diagnosed with prediabetes progresses to type 2 diabetes, and some prediabetic people actually return to normal blood glucose tolerance, so turning back the clock — when it comes to prediabetes at least — is possible. In the following sections, we cover the best methods for making this happen, including lifestyle changes and possible medications.

The evidence is inescapable: Type 2 diabetes can certainly be delayed — and even possibly be prevented — if at-risk individuals are prepared to make changes in their lifestyles and diet, and undertake drug therapy.

Modifying the lifestyle risk factors: 'The triad'

Researchers have conducted valuable studies on the prevention of type 2 diabetes, most of which confirm the benefits of increased physical activity and weight loss, as well as the benefits of using glucose-lowering drugs (namely metformin, acarbose and the thiazolidinediones). The research also suggests that people with some level of impaired glucose metabolism can certainly delay and possibly prevent the onset of diabetes, so long as they make lifestyle changes. These changes included losing 5 to 7 per cent of their body weight and increasing moderate-intensity physical activity to 150 minutes per week.

A significant finding of one study, with important implications, was that making changes in lifestyle is nearly twice as effective in prevention of developing diates as taking glucose-lowering drugs. On the other hand — but also of significance — was the study's conclusion that it's difficult to achieve these changes without intensive and costly intervention. The study's authors have now been able to assess participants ten years after the completion of the original study. Participants in the intervention group are still enjoying a significant reduction (40 per cent) in their progression to diabetes.

Tackling obesity

Many health surveys undertaken in developing countries report a significant increase in obesity over the past 10 to 15 years. Anyone who's overweight or obese has a significantly increased risk of developing diabetes. Chapter 8 gives detailed information on how you can calculate your body mass index, or BMI, and provides guidelines on reducing your weight.

If the escalating rates of obesity among adults aren't worrying enough, even more worrying is the increase in obesity in children. Increasingly, children in developing, as well as developed countries, are being diagnosed with type 2 diabetes.

Cutting kilojoules

Over the last 50 years, our energy intake has increased somewhat while our physical activity has sharply declined (the amount of exercise that the average person takes now is almost half that their parents took). While our consumption of dietary fat has increased, we're eating less fibre, fruit and vegetables. Takeaway meals, high-energy meals that are quick to prepare, and eating on the run have replaced the eating and dining habits of earlier generations.

Interestingly, in developed countries, type 2 diabetes is more prevalent at the lower socioeconomic levels of society than at the middle-class level (probably due to these people having a higher level of education as well as the time and/or finances to adopt a 'healthier' lifestyle), whereas in the developing countries, it's more prevalent among those at the upper socioeconomic levels (possibly related to the fact that the affluent have a higher kilojoule intake and are less active).

Getting physically active

In the United Kingdom, a study has shown that the level of adult obesity reflects the number of cars per household as well as the hours spent watching television. Studies conducted throughout the western world have also reported a marked decline in the number of people participating in organised sport or any physical activity.

You don't need to lose a huge amount of weight in your bid to stop your progression to diabetes — you just need to lose some! For someone who weighs 100 kilograms, losing 5 to 7 per cent body weight equates to losing just 5 to 7 kilograms.

The two best studies involving adults with prediabetes were the American Diabetes Prevention Program and the Helsinki (Finland) Study. Amazingly, in both of these studies, people with prediabetes who made changes to their lifestyle showed exactly the same reduction — 58 per cent — in progression to diabetes. These lifestyle changes were quite modest; they included participants losing 5 to 7 per cent of their body weight and undertaking 150 to 240 minutes of moderate physical activity per week.

In both the US and the Finnish studies, participants were given detailed advice from a dietitian on lowering kilojoules (see Chapter 8 for tips on improving your diet) and increasing physical activity (see Chapter 9).

As well as losing 5 to 7 per cent body weight and increasing your daily activity to 20 to 40 minutes of moderate exercise, the following factors are also effective in turning back your diabetes 'clock':

- ✔ Reducing alcohol consumption if you currently exceed two standard drinks per day
- ✔ Reducing salt in your diet to help lower your blood pressure
- ✔ Stopping smoking

Call Quitline on 131 848 or access the federal government's Quitnow website (www.quitnow.info.au) for help on giving up smoking.

Getting the family involved

Prediabetes and type 2 diabetes all have a tendency to run in families. This is partly because of an increased genetic risk in related family members, but also partly because poor diet, lack of physical activity and cigarette smoking often occur in multiple family members.

In the past, a diagnosis of any type of illness was often hidden from close friends and family. However, your, and your family's, health is more important than privacy concerns. If your family has a history of diabetes, your GP needs to know about it.

As soon as you or someone in your family gets diagnosed with prediabetes (or diabetes or gestational diabetes), inform as many close family members as possible so they can also be checked. The sooner you learn of your diabetes status, the more that can be done to avoid further health problems.

Another benefit of letting your family know about your diabetes status is that the whole crowd can then be involved in taking on a healthy lifestyle, including reducing their kilojoule intake if overweight, maintaining a good level of physical activity and avoiding smoking.

Considering medications

Researchers have found that the use of some diabetic medications may also be useful in avoiding progression from prediabetes to diabetes. These medications have been found to reduce the rate of progression to diabetes in the range of 30 to 70 per cent — not quite as good as lifestyle change!

One of the drugs used in this way has been metformin (see Chapter 7), which is at the lower end of the range in terms of effectiveness, but is the safest for long-term use.

The Australian Diabetes Society has recommended lifestyle changes alone should be the main form of treatment for prediabetes. You should only consider using medication if abnormal glucose levels persist after six months of lifestyle change.

Using metformin or other diabetic medications for prediabetes is outside the approved usage of these medications as determined by the federal government's Pharmaceutical Benefits Scheme (PBS) guidelines. This means the medications may not be available to you at the government subsidised price.

Discovering You Have Type 2 Diabetes

Rosemary Stevens, a 46-year-old woman who's 1.65 metres tall, found she weighed about 70 kilograms, which meant she had gained about 5 kilograms over a year. Rosemary had noticed that she felt more tired than usual, even though she didn't do much exercise. However, she blamed her busy lifestyle and recent weight gain for her fatigue. Another reason for Rosemary feeling more tired was that she had to get up several times a night to urinate, which was unusual for her.

Rosemary was especially disturbed because her vision had become blurry, and she did a lot of computer work. She finally went to see her GP when she developed a rash and discharge from her vagina. When Rosemary described her symptoms, her GP diagnosed thrush and decided to do a blood glucose test. Rosemary's blood glucose level that afternoon registered at 12.2 mmol/L.

Rosemary's GP asked her whether members of her family had diabetes, and she replied that her mother and a sister were both being treated for it. The doctor also asked Rosemary about any tingling in her feet, and she admitted that she had noticed some tingling for the past few months but didn't think it was important. Then her GP ordered a fasting blood glucose test from the laboratory, and it came back at 9.4 mmol/L. Rosemary's GP had to tell her that she had type 2 diabetes. Her cholesterol and trigylcerides (blood fats) were also outside the recommended range. Rosemary's GP then checked her blood pressure, which was also elevated. Her GP then explained to her that these problems — diabetes, high blood fats and a high blood pressure — were linked and were often diagnosed at the same time.

The signs and symptoms that Rosemary manifested, along with the results of the two blood glucose tests, provide a textbook picture of type 2 diabetes. (Type 2 diabetes used to be known as *non–insulin dependent diabetes mellitus* (NIDDM) or *maturity onset diabetes*.) However, people with type 2 diabetes may have few or none of these symptoms. That's why it's so important for your doctor to check your blood glucose level on a regular basis. (We discuss how often you should do this test in Chapter 6.)

Type 2 diabetes typically begins around the age of 40 and increases in frequency as you get older. However, its incidence is becoming more frequent in young children and younger adults. Because the symptoms are so mild at first, you may not notice them. You may ignore these symptoms for years before they become bothersome enough to consult your doctor. So type 2 diabetes is a disease of gradual onset rather than the severe emergency that can herald type 1 diabetes. No autoimmunity is involved in type 2 diabetes, so no antibodies are found. Doctors believe that no virus is involved in the onset of type 2 diabetes.

Recent statistics show that, throughout the world, ten times more people have type 2 diabetes than type 1. Part II tells you about the possible complications of diabetes, and Part III covers treatments that can help you prevent these complications.

Identifying the symptoms of type 2 diabetes

A fairly large percentage of the population of Australia (approximately 1.1 million people, which is equivalent to 85 per cent of all cases of diabetes) has type 2 diabetes. The following signs and symptoms are good indicators that you have type 2 diabetes. If you experience two or more of these symptoms, check with your doctor:

✔ **Fatigue:** Type 2 diabetes makes you tired because your body's cells aren't getting the glucose fuel that they need. Even though plenty of insulin is produced, your body is resistant to its actions. (Refer to Chapter 2 for further explanation.)

✔ **Frequent urination and thirst:** You find yourself urinating more frequently than usual, which dehydrates your body and leaves you thirsty.

✔ **Blurred vision:** The lenses of your eyes swell and shrink as your blood glucose levels rise and fall. Your vision blurs because your eyes can't adjust quickly enough to these changes in the lenses.

✔ **Slow healing of skin, gum and urinary infections:** Your white blood cells, which help with healing and defend your body against infections, don't function correctly in the high-glucose environment of your body when it has diabetes. Unfortunately, the bugs that cause infections thrive in the same high-glucose environment, so diabetes leaves your body especially susceptible to infections.

✔ **Genital itching:** Yeast infections also love a high-glucose environment. So diabetes is often accompanied by the itching and discomfort of yeast infections.

✔ **Numbness in the feet or legs:** You experience numbness because of a common long-term complication of diabetes, called *neuropathy*. (We explain neuropathy in Chapter 5.) If you notice numbness along with the other symptoms of diabetes, you probably have had the disease for quite a while, because neuropathy takes more than five years to develop in a person with diabetes.

✔ **Heart disease:** Heart disease occurs much more often in people with type 2 diabetes than in the non-diabetic population. However, heart disease may appear when you merely have *impaired glucose tolerance* (which we explain in the next section), before you actually have diagnosable diabetes.

✔ **Obesity:** If you're obese, you're considerably more likely to acquire diabetes than you would be if you maintained your ideal weight. (See Chapter 8 to find out how to calculate your target weight.) Not all obese people develop diabetes, however, so obesity isn't a definite indication of diabetes.

Investigating the causes of type 2 diabetes

Although type 2 diabetes doesn't usually appear in your body until later in life, if you've been diagnosed with type 2 diabetes, you're probably nonetheless shocked and curious about why you developed the disease. Doctors have learnt quite a bit about the causes of type 2 diabetes. For example, they know that type 2 diabetes runs in families. Usually, people with type 2 diabetes can find a relative who has had the disease. Therefore, doctors consider type 2 diabetes to be much more of a genetic disease than type 1 diabetes.

In studies of identical twins, when one twin has type 2 diabetes, the likelihood that type 2 diabetes will develop in the other twin is between 75 and 90 per cent. A number of ongoing studies are investigating the susceptibility genes associated with the development of type 2 diabetes.

Developing insulin resistance

People with type 2 diabetes have plenty of insulin in their bodies but their bodies respond to the insulin in abnormal ways. Those with type 2 diabetes are *insulin-resistant*, meaning that their bodies resist the normal, healthy functioning of insulin. This insulin resistance, combined with not producing enough insulin to overcome the insulin resistance, causes type 2 diabetes.

Even before obesity sets in, or the person does no exercise, or diabetes is present, future type 2 patients already show signs of insulin resistance. First of all, the level of insulin in the blood of these people is elevated compared to the level found in normal people. Secondly, an injection of insulin doesn't reduce the blood glucose in these insulin-resistant people nearly as much as it does in people without insulin resistance. (See Chapter 7 for more about insulin injections in diabetes.)

When your body needs to make extra insulin just to keep your blood glucose normal, your insulin is, obviously, less effective than it should be — which means that you have *impaired glucose tolerance* or *prediabetes* (refer to the section 'Diagnosing Prediabetes' for more information). Your body goes through impaired glucose tolerance before you actually have diabetes, because your blood glucose is still lower than the levels needed for a diagnosis of diabetes (refer to Chapter 2). When you have impaired glucose tolerance and you add other factors such as weight gain, a sedentary lifestyle or ageing, your pancreas can't keep up with your insulin demands and you develop diabetes.

Another factor that comes into play when doctors make a diagnosis of type 2 diabetes is the release of sugar from your liver, known as your *hepatic glucose output*. Why is your glucose high in the morning after you've fasted all night if you have type 2 diabetes? You would think that your glucose would be low because you haven't eaten any sugar that would increase your body's glucose. In fact, your liver is a storage bank for a lot of glucose, and it can make even more from other substances in the body. As your insulin resistance increases, your liver begins to release glucose inappropriately and your fasting blood glucose rises.

Dispelling myths about the causes of type 2 diabetes

People often think that the following factors cause type 2 diabetes, but they actually have nothing to do with the onset of the disease:

- **Antibodies:** Antibodies against islet cells aren't a major factor in type 2 diabetes. Type 2 diabetes isn't an autoimmune disease like type 1.

- **Diabetic ketoacidosis:** Type 2 diabetes isn't generally associated with diabetic ketoacidosis. People with type 2 diabetes are ketosis-resistant, except under extremely severe stress caused by infections or trauma. (Also see Chapter 4 for a discussion of *hyperglycaemic hyperosmolar state*, a related condition in which people with type 2 diabetes have extremely high glucose but don't have the fat breakdown that leads to ketoacidosis.)

- **Emotions:** Changes in your emotions don't play a large role in the development of type 2 diabetes, but may be very important in dealing with diabetes mellitus and subsequent control.

- **Gender:** Males and females are equally as likely to develop type 2 diabetes. Gender doesn't play a role in the onset of this disease.

- **Stress:** Too much stress isn't a major cause of diabetes.

- **Sugar:** Eating excessive amounts of sugar doesn't cause diabetes — although it may bring out the disease to the extent that it makes you fat. Eating too much protein or fat does the same thing.

Thanks for shopping with us.
Kindest Regards, Customer Care

RETURNING GOODS

Please re-pack, in the original packaging if possible, and send back to us at the address below. **Caution!** Don't cover up the barcode (on original packaging) as it helps us to process your return.

We will email you when we have processed your return.

---------------------------✂---

PLEASE complete and include this section with your goods.

Your Name: _____

Your Order Number _____

Reason for return _____

Select: Refund my order ☐   Replace my order ☐

(Please note, if we are unable to replace the item it will be refunded.)

Return to:
---------------------------✂---

RETURNS
Unit 22, Horcott Industrial Estate
Horcott Road
FAIRFORD
GL7 4BX

Part II

How Type 2 Diabetes Affects Your Body

Glenn Lumsden

'Maybe it'd be quicker if you listed the bits that aren't affected by diabetes.'

In this part ...

*T*ype 2 diabetes, if not treated properly, can have profound effects on your body. This part explains these effects, how they occur, the kinds of symptoms they produce, and what you and your doctor need to do to treat them. You may be surprised at how many parts of your body can be affected by diabetes. Remember that many things described in this part are preventable — and even if you haven't been able to prevent type 2 diabetes, it is very treatable.

Medical research has resulted in great advances in the treatment of diabetes. While many of the effects of the disease may be reduced or even eliminated in the not-too-distant future, you need to know about the effects and respond to them appropriately.

Chapter 4

Managing Short-Term Ailments

. . . .

In This Chapter

▶ Understanding the complications involved with short-term illness

▶ Managing your health while battling colds and other sicknesses

▶ Dealing with low blood glucose

▶ Coping with the highest blood glucose

. . . .

Chapter 2 tells you how doctors make a diagnosis of type 2 diabetes, and covers some of the signs and symptoms of diabetes, which you could consider to be the shortest of the short-term problems of the disease because they're generally mild and begin to subside when you start treatment. This chapter covers the more serious forms of short-term issues of diabetes management, which occur when your blood glucose is out of control — reaching uncomfortably high or low levels. We refer to these events as the 'lumps and bumps of diabetes'.

 With the exception of mild *hypoglycaemia* (low blood glucose), you should treat all the complications described in this chapter as medical emergencies. Keep in touch with your doctor or diabetes educator when the symptoms are mild, and go to hospital promptly if your blood glucose is uncontrollably high or you're unable to hold down food. You may need a few hours in the emergency department or a day or two in hospital to reverse your problems.

Solving Short-Term Problems

Although the problems covered in this chapter are called *short term*, you may experience them at any time during the course of your diabetes. *Short term* simply means that these conditions arise rapidly in your body, as opposed to the long-term complications that take years to develop. (See Chapter 5 for the details of long-term complications.) Short-term problems develop in days or even hours and, fortunately, they respond to treatment just as rapidly.

The short-term problems of diabetes like low blood glucose levels (hypoglycaemia) may affect your ability to function normally. You may find that the authority that governs road safety and driver licensing in your state (such as the Road Transport Authority in New South Wales or VicRoads in Victoria) and the Civil Aviation Safety Authority (CASA) are more careful about giving you, and all people with diabetes, a driver's licence or a pilot's licence. Potential employers may question your ability to perform certain jobs. But most companies and government departments are very enlightened about diabetes and do everything possible to accommodate you in these situations. (Contact the Australian Diabetes Council (in NSW) or Diabetes Australia in other states or territories if you feel that you have been discriminated against because of your diabetes.)

You don't have to feel limited in what you can do. You can have control over your diabetes, and the short-term problems are manageable. If you closely monitor and control your blood glucose, you can quickly determine any drop to lower than normal levels or elevations to higher than normal levels, and you can treat these problems before they affect your mental and physical functioning. (See Chapter 6 for details on glucose monitoring and other testing.)

Coping With Colds and Other Nasties

Everyone comes down with a mild illness or virus once in a while. For most people, even those with diabetes, these illnesses cause them some inconvenience and maybe a few days away from work. However, for some people with diabetes, even a mild illness can cause problems with their blood glucose levels. When you're unwell with a virus such as the common cold, your immune system is fighting to destroy the virus and make you well again. Stress hormones are also increased at this time and these can make your body more resistant to insulin, which makes your blood glucose levels rise. They may rise a little or quite a lot — each time is slightly different.

In the following sections, we cover ways you can manage your health while sick with minor illnesses, and highlight what you need to be most aware of.

 Your diabetes care team may refer to the occasions of illness as 'sick days' and can discuss strategies for sick-day management with you.

Being prepared for sick days

When you come down with a virus like the common cold or influenza, you hardly feel at the top of your game, so it pays to know how to cope with illness *before* you get sick. If you have a short-term illness you should

- ✔ **Get plenty of rest**

- ✔ **Drink plenty of fluids** — sugar free if your blood glucose levels are normal or high; sweet if your blood glucose levels are low

- ✔ **Eat a little and often** — avoid spicy and fatty foods, especially if you have an upset stomach

- ✔ **Keep taking your insulin or tablets** — even if you're hardly eating, continue to take your prescribed medications because your body still needs them all

- ✔ **Contact your doctor if the illness persists** — call your GP if you're still feeling sick after a few days or if you seem to be getting worse rather than better

 Put together a 'sick day' kit that contains a range of items for when you're unwell, and keep it stocked up and easily accessible. Here's a list of items to keep in your sick day kit:

- ✔ Blood glucose test strips (check they're not past their expiry dates)

- ✔ Cans of ordinary lemonade (or equivalent)

- ✔ Contact details of your local doctor, endocrinologist, local diabetes centre, and/or after-hours medical service

✔ Pain relief

✔ Sachets of oral rehydration solution

✔ Sick Day information booklet (published by the Australian Diabetes Educators Association and available from your diabetes team)

✔ Small packet of plain biscuits, such as crackers or sweet biscuits

✔ Thermometer

Monitoring glucose

When battling illness, many people with diabetes monitor their blood glucose levels less frequently because they 'know it will be high anyway' or 'just feel too sick to test'. Unfortunately, failing to monitor your glucose levels when unwell can make things worse so continue to test at your usual frequency (see Chapter 6 for more on blood glucose and other testing). If you notice that the levels are getting higher, start to test more often to see if they're continuing to get higher.

If you're testing your blood glucose levels and regularly getting levels greater than 14 mmol/L, or you have a significant increase in your thirst or urination, contact your doctor or diabetes service for advice.

Knowing what to eat and drink

As someone with diabetes, you've probably been told how important it is to eat regular meals. However, when you're sick, you may not be interested in food at all — or, worse, you might have a nasty diarrhoea and vomiting bug, and can't keep much down. Don't worry — illness isn't your usual state, so the requirement to eat regular meals doesn't necessarily apply. What becomes most important is that you drink plenty of fluids throughout the day.

Our bodies absorb fluids containing small amounts of sugar and salt better than plain water alone, so drink a mixture of slightly sweet fluids, such as weak cordial or diluted fruit juice, and slightly salty fluids, such as clear broth or consommé or Vegemite mixed with hot water. Alternatively, you can use sachets of oral re-hydration solution (available from the chemist) to make drinks or iceblocks.

Drink small amounts often. Drinking 250 millilitres should take you about one hour.

Contacting important people

Managing your blood glucose levels when you're feeling unwell can be difficult — particularly if it's the first time you've been sick since being diagnosed with diabetes. And while having a poor intake of food causes little damage to your body over only a few days, the lack of food becomes more troublesome if a short-term illness turns into something more serious and long term.

If your blood glucose levels are rising and you're not getting better, call your GP or diabetes care team. Some advice and reassurance from them may be all that you need, and they can also assist you in managing the situation at home — or they may recommend a trip to the hospital if they believe the situation is more serious. If it's out-of-hours, go to the emergency department of your local hospital or call the after-hours line for your local diabetes centre.

Understanding Hypoglycaemia

The condition of low blood glucose is known as *hypoglycaemia*. If you have diabetes, you can get hypoglycaemia only as a consequence of your diabetes treatment.

Hypoglycaemia is much less common in people with type 2 diabetes than in those with type 1 diabetes. It can only occur in someone taking sulphonylureas or insulin. So while most people with type 2 diabetes never experience hypoglycaemia, we've included information about hypogylcaemia in this chapter just to be on the safe side.

As a person with diabetes, you're in constant combat with *high* blood glucose, which is responsible for most of the long-term and short-term complications of the disease. Your doctor prescribes drugs and other treatments in an effort to finetune your blood glucose as it would be in someone else's body. (Part III explains many techniques that help you to control your blood glucose levels.) But, unfortunately, these drugs and treatments aren't always perfect. If you take too much of a drug, exercise too much or eat too little, or you become suddenly unwell, your blood glucose can drop to the low levels at which symptoms develop — and this can occur in both type 1 and type 2 diabetes. The following sections explain more about hypoglycaemia's symptoms, causes and treatment.

Getting acquainted with the signs and symptoms

Your body doesn't function well when you have too little glucose in your blood. Your brain needs glucose to run the rest of your body, as well as for intellectual purposes. Your muscles need the energy that glucose provides in much the same way that your car needs petrol. So, when your body detects that it has low blood glucose, it sends out a group of hormones that rapidly raise your glucose. But those hormones have to fight the strength of the diabetes medication that has been pushing down your glucose levels.

At what level of blood glucose do you develop hypoglycaemic symptoms? Unfortunately, the level varies for different individuals, particularly depending on the length of time that the person has had diabetes. But most experts agree that a blood glucose of less than 4.0 mmol/L is associated with signs and symptoms of hypoglycaemia in most diabetic people.

Doctors traditionally put the symptoms of hypoglycaemia into two major categories:

- ✓ **Symptoms that are due to your brain not receiving enough fuel so that your intellectual function suffers.** This first category of symptoms is called *neuroglycopaenic* symptoms, which is medical talk for 'not enough (*paenic*) glucose (*glyco*) in the brain (*neuro*)'. (If your brain could speak, it would just say, 'Whew, I need a feed!')

- ✓ **Symptoms due to the side effects of the hormones (especially adrenaline) that your body sends out to mobilise glucose into your bloodstream.** The second category of symptoms is called adrenergic symptoms, because adrenaline, a stress hormone, comes from your adrenal gland.

Adrenergic symptoms occur most often when your blood glucose falls rapidly. These symptoms are often the first sign of hypoglycaemia, and serve as a warning that you need to check your glucose level and treat yourself if it is low.

The following adrenergic symptoms may warn you that you're hypoglycaemic:

- ✔ Anxiety
- ✔ Palpitations, or the feeling that your heart is beating too fast
- ✔ Rapid heartbeat
- ✔ Sensation of hunger
- ✔ Sweating
- ✔ Whiteness, or pallor, of your skin

Neuroglycopaenic symptoms occur most often when your hypoglycaemia takes longer to develop. The symptoms become more severe as your blood glucose drops lower and you will require urgent medical attention. The following neuroglycopaenic symptoms are often signs that you're becoming (or already are) hypoglycaemic:

- ✔ Confusion
- ✔ Fatigue
- ✔ Headache
- ✔ Irritation
- ✔ Loss of concentration
- ✔ Visual disorders, such as double vision

People lose their ability to think clearly when they become hypoglycaemic. They make simple mistakes, and other people may assume that they're drunk.

One of our patients was driving on a freeway when a police officer noticed that she was weaving back and forth in her lane and pulled her over. He concluded that she was drunk and took her to the police station. Fortunately, someone noticed that she was wearing a medical alert bracelet engraved with her diabetes details. After promptly receiving the nutrition that she needed, she rapidly recovered. No charges were laid, but clearly this is a situation that you want to avoid. Always test your blood glucose level to make sure that it's satisfactory before driving your car.

If you take insulin or a *sulphonylurea drug*, which squeezes more insulin out of your reluctant pancreas, for your own safety you need to wear or carry with you some form of identification, in case you unexpectedly develop hypoglycaemia. You should also carry with you information regarding your diagnosis, a list of your current medications and the contact details for your doctor or a family member, in case you are unable to communicate. (See Chapter 7 for a full explanation of the insulin and sulphonylurea medications.)

Knowing the causes

Hypoglycaemia results from elevated amounts of insulin driving down your blood glucose to low levels, but a too high dose of insulin or sulphonylurea isn't always the culprit that causes hypoglycaemia. The amount of food you take in, the amount of fuel (glucose) that you burn during activity, the rate of insulin disposal by your body and your body's ability to release glucose from the liver or make it from other body substances all affect your blood glucose level.

Insulin and sulphonylurea drugs

When you have insulin injections, you have to time your food intake to raise your blood glucose as the insulin is taking effect. Chapter 7 explains the different kinds of insulin and the proper methods for administering them. But remember that the various types of insulin differ in maximum effect (minutes or hours) after you inject them. If you miss a meal or take your insulin too early or too late, your glucose and insulin levels won't be in sync and you'll develop hypoglycaemia. If you go on a diet and don't lower your medication, the same thing happens.

When taking insulin, mistakes can happen. Sometimes hypoglycaemia results from taking the wrong dose or the wrong type of insulin, so even if you've been taking insulin for many years, still double-check what you are taking every time you take it.

If you take sulphonylurea drugs, you need to follow similar precautions. You and your doctor must adjust your dosage when your kilojoule intake falls. Other drugs, such as metformin, don't cause hypoglycaemia by themselves, but when combined with sulphonylureas may lower your glucose enough to reach hypoglycaemic levels. (Chapter 7 talks more about these other drugs.)

Diet

Your diet plays a role in helping you to avoid hypoglycaemia if you take medication. You usually need to eat breakfast, lunch and dinner at regular times each day.

When you need to eat meals, and how much you should eat at each meal, differs depending on the type of insulin you take. Always discuss your need (or lack thereof) for meals and any snacks with your diabetes dietitian when starting insulin or changing the type or dose you take.

Most people with type 2 diabetes don't need to eat snacks to prevent hypoglycaemia. If you're regularly experiencing hypoglycaemia, discuss this situation with your GP, endocrinologist or diabetes care team — it may be your medication that needs adjustment, rather than your diet.

Chapter 8 gives much greater detail about how you can best manage your individual dietary needs.

Exercise

Exercise burns more of your body's fuel, which is primarily glucose, so it lowers your blood glucose. Some people with diabetes use exercise in place of extra insulin to get their high blood glucose down to a normal level. However, if you don't adjust your insulin dose or food intake to match your exercise, exercise may result in hypoglycaemia.

People who exercise regularly require less medication and generally can manage their diabetes more easily than non-exercisers can. Talk to your diabetes care team about how best to fit exercise into your life. (See Chapter 9 for more on the benefits of exercise.)

Non-diabetes medications

Several drugs that you may take unrelated to your diabetes can lower your blood glucose. One important and widely used drug, which you may not even think of as a drug, is alcohol (in the form of wine, beer and spirits). Alcohol can block your liver's ability to release glucose. It also blocks hormones that raise blood glucose and increases the glucose-lowering effect of insulin. If you drink alcohol on an empty stomach, or before going to bed, you may experience severe hypoglycaemia overnight or the next morning. While this is more common in those people with type 1 diabetes, those with type 2 may also notice this effect.

Watch out for these drugs that can lower your blood glucose:

 ✔ **Alcohol:** If you take insulin or sulphonylurea drugs, don't drink alcohol without eating some food at the same time. Food counteracts some of the glucose-lowering effects of alcohol.

 ✔ **Aspirin:** Aspirin (and all the drugs related to aspirin, called *salicylates*) can lead to hypoglycaemia if used in high doses (greater than 300 milligrams per day). In adults who have diabetes, aspirin can increase the effects of other drugs that you're taking to lower your blood glucose. In children with diabetes, aspirin has an especially profound effect on lowering blood glucose to hypoglycaemia levels.

Treating the problem

To treat hypoglycaemia, the first step should always be to check your blood glucose level with your glucometer when you suspect you may be experiencing hypoglycaemia. Some of the symptoms of hypoglycaemia we have described can be a result of other things (for example, it's a hot day, you haven't had enough to eat or drink, your blood pressure is too low and so on). So, before you start treating your symptoms check your glucose levels and only proceed if your glucose is 4mmol/l or under!

The vast majority of hypoglycaemia cases are mild. If you (or a friend or relative) notice that you have the early symptoms of hypoglycaemia, you can treat the problem with a small quantity of glucose in the form of

 ✔ Pre-packaged sachet of glucose gel

 ✔ Six to eight jelly beans

 ✔ Three glucose tablets (available from chemists)

 ✔ Three small sugar cubes or sachets

 ✔ 150 millilitres (or about half a cup) of a sugary soft drink or fruit juice

Sometimes you need a second treatment. Approximately ten minutes after you try one of these solutions, measure your blood glucose to find out whether your level has risen sufficiently. If it's still low, again take one of the forms of glucose in the preceding list.

This fast-acting glucose only lasts a short time, and within the next hour you need to eat another small serve of a carbohydrate source such as a piece of fruit, a slice of bread or two plain sweet biscuits, in addition to the initial glucose treatment, in order to prevent further lowering of blood glucose levels. Continue to monitor your glucose levels and watch for further signs of hypoglycaemia, as some insulins can have a long duration of effect.

Because your mental state may be mildly confused when you have hypoglycaemia, you need to make sure that your friends or relatives know in advance what hypoglycaemia is and what to do about it. Inform people about your diabetes and about how to recognise hypoglycaemia. Don't keep your diabetes a secret. The people close to you will be glad to know how to help you.

If you can't sit up and swallow properly when you have hypoglycaemia, people shouldn't try to feed you, as this may cause more harm. If your hypoglycaemia doesn't respond to treatment and you remain in a state of reduced conciousness with a very low blood glucose level, the person helping you needs to make an emergency 000 call. The ambulance officers check your blood glucose and give you an intravenous (IV) dose of high-concentration glucose. Most likely, you continue the IV in the emergency department until you show stable and normal blood glucose levels.

After a case of hypoglycaemia — and after the sweat has dried and the shakes have gone — it's a good idea to sit down and think about why this condition might have occurred. Could it have been related to food, alcohol, exercise or incorrect insulin dose? Or are you just not sure? Contact your GP or diabetes care team to discuss possible causes of your hypoglycaemia and how you can prevent it happening again.

Managing Hyperglycaemic Hyperosmolar State

In people with type 2 diabetes, high blood glucose levels can lead you to a condition known as *hyperglycaemic hyperosmolar state* (HHS). This condition is a medical emergency that needs to be treated in a hospital.

The term hyperglycaemic hyperosmolar state refers to the excessive levels of glucose in the blood. Hyper means 'larger than normal', and osmolar has to do with concentrations of substances in the blood. So hyperosmolar, in this situation, means that the blood is simply too highly concentrated with glucose. Other hyperosmolar syndromes occur when other substances are excessive.

The following sections explain the symptoms, causes and treatments for HHS.

Seeing the symptoms

If you measure your blood glucose on a daily basis, you should never develop HHS because you're able to notice that your blood glucose is getting high before it reaches a critical level. The most important signs and symptoms of HHS are as follows:

- Blood glucose of 33.3 mmol/L, or even higher if you wait too long to seek medical help
- Decreased mental awareness or coma
- Frequent urination
- Leg cramps
- Sunken eyeballs and rapid pulse, due to dehydration
- Thirst
- Weakness

You may also develop more threatening symptoms with this complication. Your blood pressure may be low and your nervous system may be affected with stroke-like effects that respond to treatment. You may have high counts of sodium and other blood constituents (such as white blood cells and red blood cells). With treatment, these counts usually fall rapidly and your doctor replaces these elements in your blood as water is restored to your body. Treatment needs to start quickly, however, so seek medical assistance immediately if you experience more than one of the symptoms in the preceding list.

Finding the causes

HHS is more likely to occur in people with diabetes who live alone or in those whose diabetes hasn't been carefully monitored. These people may have mild type 2 diabetes that perhaps has been previously undiagnosed and/or untreated.

Age is also a contributing cause of HHS because your kidneys gradually become less efficient as you age. When your kidneys are in their prime, your blood glucose level needs to reach only 10 mmol/L before your kidneys begin to remove some excess glucose through your urine. But as your kidneys grow older, they require a gradually higher blood glucose level before they start to send excess glucose to your urine. If you're at an age (usually 70 or older for people in average health) when your kidneys are really labouring to remove the excess glucose from your body and you happen to lose a large amount of fluids from sickness, your blood volume decreases, which makes it even harder for your kidneys to remove glucose. At this point, your blood glucose level begins to skyrocket. If you don't replace some of the lost fluids soon, your glucose rises even higher.

If you allow your blood glucose to rise and you don't get the fluids you need, your blood pressure starts to fall and you get weaker and weaker. As the concentration of glucose in your blood continues to rise, you become increasingly confused. Your mental state diminishes as the glucose concentration rises until you eventually fall into a coma.

Other factors — such as infection, failure to take your insulin, and taking certain medications — can raise your blood glucose to HHS levels; however, not replacing lost body fluids is the most frequent cause.

Remedying hyperglycaemic hyperosmolar state

HHS requires immediate and skilled treatment from a doctor. By no means should you try to treat HHS yourself. You need the proper treatment from an experienced doctor — and you need it fast. The death rate for HHS is high because many of the people who develop it are elderly and often have other serious illnesses that complicate treatment.

When you arrive at your doctor's surgery or at the emergency department with HHS, your doctor must accomplish the following tasks fairly rapidly:

- ✔ Restore large volumes of water to your body

- ✔ Lower your blood glucose level

- ✔ Restore other substances that your body has lost, such as sodium, chloride, potassium and so on

Your doctor creates a chart to monitor your levels of glucose, blood concentration (osmolarity), potassium, sodium and other tests, which are measured hourly in some cases. You may think that you need to receive large amounts of insulin to lower your high glucose level, but the large doses of fluids that your doctor gives you do so much to lower your glucose that you need only smaller doses of insulin. As your body fluids return to normal, your kidneys begin to receive much more of the blood that they need in order to rid your body of the excess glucose.

If you're unfortunate enough to experience HHS, after you have recovered, consider which factors may have caused the problem and how you can avoid it happening again. For example, did you stop testing your blood glucose levels, stop taking your tablets or put off seeing your doctor when feeling unwell? Discuss possible causes with your doctor and diabetes care team.

Chapter 5

Preventing Long-Term Complications

. . . .

In This Chapter

▶ Understanding the effects of diabetes on your heart and arteries

▶ Keeping your cholesterol and blood pressure under control

▶ Dealing with kidney disease

▶ Handling problems with your eyes

▶ Battling damage to your nerves

▶ Looking after your feet

▶ Rectifying problems with sexual function

▶ Identifying skin complaints

. . . .

*C*omplications can occur if your blood glucose rises and remains high over many years. Two types of complications are associated with long-term poor blood glucose control: *Macrovascular* disease, which affects the heart and other major blood vessels, such as those to the legs and the brain, and *microvascular* disease, which affects the eyes, kidneys and nerves.

Doctors believe that years of high blood glucose levels initiate most of the long-term complications of diabetes — such as kidney disease, eye disease and nerve disease. Heart disease is an exception because high blood glucose levels may make the disease worse or more complicated but not actually cause it.

Most long-term complications require five or more years to develop, which seems like a long time until you consider that many people with type 2 diabetes have had it for five or more years before a doctor diagnoses it. Often the long-term complication itself (rather than a high blood glucose level) is the clue that leads a doctor to diagnose type 2 diabetes in a patient. Doctors need to look for long-term complications immediately after diagnosing type 2 diabetes.

In this chapter, we take a look at the major long-term complications and how you can best deal with them. The point that we stress throughout this book is that you have a choice: If you work with your doctor and diabetes care team, you can keep your blood glucose near normal, and you may never have to deal with any long-term complications.

Fighting Heart Disease

In the last three decades, the number of deaths due to heart disease has fallen dramatically, thanks to all kinds of new treatments. Unfortunately, a tremendous increase in the number of people with type 2 diabetes is predicted for the next few decades, which may reverse this trend. In this section, you find out about the special problems that diabetes brings to the heart.

Risks of heart disease to people with diabetes

Coronary artery disease (ischaemic heart disease) is the term for the progressive closure of the arteries that supply blood to the heart muscle (atherosclerosis). When one or more of your arteries closes completely, the result is a heart attack (myocardial infarction). Coronary Artery Disease (CAD) is the most common reason for death in people with type 2 diabetes. Many risk factors promote CAD in the type 2 person, including the following:

- **Abnormal blood fats**, especially reduced HDL and increased triglyceride. (See the section 'Tracking Cholesterol and Other Fats' later in this chapter for more.) People with impaired glucose tolerance may also show the same abnormalities.

- **Central adiposity**, which refers to the distribution of fat particularly in the waist area.

- **Hypertension** (high blood pressure).

- **Obesity**, often due to lack of exercise and a high-fat diet.

In addition to the known risk factors, unknown cardiovascular risk factors are related to insulin resistance itself. People with diabetes have more CAD than people without diabetes. When X-ray studies of the heart blood vessels are compared, people with diabetes have more arteries involved than people without diabetes.

If a heart attack occurs, the risk of death is much greater for the person with diabetes. Fifty per cent of people with diabetes die from coronary heart disease compared to 23 per cent of the population without diabetes. The death rate is worse for the person with diabetes who was in poor glucose control before the heart attack. The same poorly controlled person has more complications, such as heart failure, from a heart attack than the person without diabetes. Once a heart attack occurs, the outlook is much worse for the person with diabetes. The death rate five years after the heart attack is 50 per cent, compared with 25 per cent in people without diabetes. People with diabetes commonly *don't* get chest pain when they have a heart attack due to nerve damage and this may be one reason why people may not get the treatment they need when they need it.

The picture isn't a pretty one for the person with diabetes who has coronary artery disease. The treatment options are the same for people with or without diabetes. Treatment to dissolve the clot of blood obstructing the coronary artery can be used, but people with diabetes don't do as well with *angioplasty and stenting*, the technique by which a tube is placed into the artery to clean it out and open it up.

People with diabetes do as well with surgery to bypass the obstruction (called *bypass surgery*) as do people without diabetes, but the long-term prognosis for keeping the graft open isn't as good.

Keeping a finger on the pulse

Three main conditions caused by diabetes can have an effect on the heart:

- ✔ **Metabolic syndrome:** The earliest abnormality in type 2 diabetes is insulin resistance, known as metabolic syndrome, syndrome X or insulin resistance syndrome. The syndrome is accompanied by several features, including abnormal blood fats, hypertension, increased abdominal visceral fat, increased plasminogen activator inhibitor-1, obesity and sedentary lifestyle.

The preceding features, plus other features not listed, are found in people who have an increased tendency to suffer coronary artery disease and heart attacks. Keep in mind that the condition is present even when diabetes is not.

For further information on metabolic syndrome and its treatments, refer to *Diabetes For Dummies*, *3rd Australian Edition*.

✔ **Cardiac autonomic neuropathy:** Basically, the heart is under the control of nerves, and high glucose levels can damage these nerves. The presence of cardiac autonomic neuropathy results in a diminished survival even when no coronary artery disease is present. You can test for cardiac autonomic neuropathy by measuring the resting heart rate, the standing blood pressure and the variation in heart rate between when you breathe in and when you breathe out.

✔ **Cardiomyopathy:** This refers to an enlarged heart and scarring of the heart muscle in the absence of coronary artery disease. The heart doesn't pump enough blood with each stroke. The person may be able to compensate with a more rapid heart rate, but if hypertension is present, a stable condition can deteriorate. The key treatment in this condition is control of the blood pressure as well as control of the blood glucose. Studies in animals in which diabetic cardiomyopathy is induced have shown healing with control of the blood glucose.

Other Diseases of the Vascular System

The same processes that affect the coronary arteries (refer to the section 'Risks of heart disease to people with diabetes' earlier in this chapter) can affect the arteries to the rest of the body, producing peripheral vascular disease, and the arteries to the brain, producing cerebrovascular disease.

Peripheral vascular disease

Peripheral vascular disease (PVD) occurs much earlier in someone with diabetes than in someone without diabetes, and proceeds more rapidly. The clogging of the arteries results in loss of pulses in the feet so that at the time of diagnosis of type 2 diabetes, 8 per cent of men and women no longer feel a pulse in their feet; after 20 years of diabetes, the percentage rises to 45. People with PVD also have a reduction in life expectancy. When PVD occurs, it's much worse in people with diabetes who have much greater involvement of arteries, just as in the heart.

Many risk factors increase the severity of PVD, a couple of which are unavoidable, as follows:

- ✔ **Age**, because the risk of PVD increases as you age

- ✔ **Genetic factors**, because PVD is more common in some families and certain ethnic groups

Take action now to tackle those risk factors that can be successfully eliminated. You need to address the following:

- ✔ **High glucose**, which you can control

- ✔ **Hypercholesterolaemia (high cholesterol)**, which makes PVD worse

- ✔ **Hypertension**, which you can control with tablets if necessary

- ✔ **Obesity**, which you can control

- ✔ **Smoking**, which studies show clearly leads to early amputation and which you can control

In addition to taking action yourself to control or eliminate some of these factors, you can take advantage of certain drugs. Some drugs help prevent closure of the arteries and loss of blood supply — aspirin, which inhibits clotting, is among the most useful.

Cerebrovascular disease

Cerebrovascular disease (CVD) is disease of the arteries that supply the brain with oxygen and nutrients. The risk factors and approach to treatment for cerebrovascular disease are somewhat similar to those for peripheral vascular disease (see preceding section). However, the symptoms are very different because the clogged arteries in CVD supply the brain. If a temporary reduction in blood supply to the brain occurs, the person suffers from a *transient ischaemic attack*, or TIA. This temporary loss of brain function may present itself as slurring of speech, weakness on one side of the body, or numbness. A TIA may disappear after a few minutes, but it comes back again some hours or days later. If a major artery to the brain completely closes, the person suffers a stroke. Fortunately, stroke victims who get medical assistance soon after a stroke can take advantage of clot-dissolving medications.

People with diabetes are at increased risk for CVD just as they are for PVD, and their experience of CVD tends to be worse than it is for the person without diabetes. People with diabetes can suffer from blockage in many small blood vessels in the brain with loss of intellectual function, which is similar to Alzheimer's disease.

Tracking Cholesterol and Other Fats

These days most people are aware of their cholesterol levels — actually, what they know is the level of their *total* cholesterol. Cholesterol circulates in the blood in small packages called *lipoproteins*. These tiny round particles contain fat (*lipo*, as in liposuction) and protein. Because cholesterol doesn't dissolve in water, it would separate from the blood if it weren't surrounded by the protein, just like oil separates from vinegar in salad dressing.

A second kind of fat found in the lipoproteins is *triglyceride*. Triglyceride actually represents the form of most of the fat you eat each day. Although you probably eat only a gram or less of cholesterol (an egg yolk is one-third of a gram of cholesterol), you may eat up to 100 grams of triglyceride per day. (For more on the place of fats in your diet, see Chapter 8.) The fat in animal meats is mostly triglycerides.

When you have your cholesterol checked, find out which particle the cholesterol comes from so that you know whether you have too much bad cholesterol (LDL) or a satisfactory level of good cholesterol (HDL).

Studies show that the risk for coronary artery disease goes up as the LDL cholesterol rises and the HDL cholesterol falls. A study of thousands of people from Framingham, Massachusetts, in the United States, showed that you can get a good picture of the risk by dividing the total cholesterol by the HDL cholesterol.

If this result is less than 4.5, the risk is lower. If it's more than 4.5, you're at higher risk of coronary artery disease — and the higher it is, the greater the risk.

The Australian National Heart Foundation deems people with diabetes to be a high-risk group for coronary artery disease. Table 5-1 shows the Heart Foundation's recommended target fat values for people with diabetes.

Table 5-1	Target Fat Levels for People with Diabetes			
	Total Cholesterol	*Triglycerides*	*HDL*	*LDL*
Fasting plasma concentration (mmol/L)	<4	<2	≥1	<2.5

In considering the best treatment for you as regards fat levels, you have to consider other risk factors. You're at

- ✔ Highest risk if you already have coronary artery disease, stroke or peripheral vascular disease

- ✔ High risk if you

  - Are a male over 45

  - Are a female over 55

  - Smoke cigarettes

  - Have high blood pressure

  - Have HDL cholesterol less than 1 mmol/L

  - Have a father or brother who had a heart attack before age 55

  - Have a mother or sister who had a heart attack before age 65

  - Have a body mass index greater than 30

- ✔ Lower risk if you have none of the preceding risk factors

The treatment then depends on your risk category and level of LDL cholesterol. If you have already had a heart attack, the target for LDL may be lower (that is, less than 2 mmol/L).

Measuring Blood Pressure

Australia is experiencing an epidemic of high blood pressure (*hypertension*) similar to the epidemic of diabetes. The reasons are the same:

✔ Australians are getting fatter. An Australian study has shown that 60 per cent of Australian adults are either obese or overweight, and a slightly larger proportion of this group is male.

✔ Australians are storing fat in the centre of their bodies, the so-called *abdominal visceral fat*.

✔ The population of Australia is ageing — the fastest-growing segment of the population is over 65 years of age. Of people with diabetes, older people have a higher risk of having hypertension.

✔ Australians are more sedentary than before.

People with diabetes have high blood pressure more often than people without diabetes for many reasons besides the preceding ones. For instance, they

✔ Are prone to kidney disease

✔ Have increased sensitivity to salt, a substance that raises blood pressure

✔ Don't experience the nightly fall in blood pressure that normally occurs in people without diabetes

Normal blood pressure is less than 130/85. (The upper reading is known as the *systolic pressure*, while the lower reading is known as the *diastolic blood pressure*.) For years, the diastolic blood pressure was considered more damaging, but recent studies have shown that it's the systolic blood pressure, not the diastolic blood pressure that may be more important. A recent study (the ADVANCE trial) showed that treatment of high blood pressure in people with type 2 diabetes resulted in a 14 per cent reduction in death and an 18 per cent reduction in death from heart attack.

All the complications of diabetes are made worse by an elevation in blood pressure, especially diabetic kidney disease, but also eye disease, heart disease, nerve disease, peripheral vascular disease and cerebral arterial disease. Controlling the blood pressure is absolutely essential in diabetes.

Your doctor should measure your blood pressure at every visit. Better still, get a blood pressure device and measure it yourself. Your blood pressure should be no higher than 140/90; if you have kidney disease, it should be even lower. If you detect an elevation, bring it to the attention of your doctor.

Controlling Kidney Disease

Your kidneys rid your body of many harmful chemicals and other compounds produced during the process of normal metabolism. Your kidneys act like a filter through which your blood pours, trapping the waste and sending it out in your urine, while the normal contents of the blood go back into your bloodstream. Kidneys also regulate the salt and water content of your body. When kidney disease (also known as *nephropathy*) causes your kidneys to fail, you must either use artificial means, called *dialysis*, to cleanse your blood and control the salt and water, or you may receive a new working donor kidney, called a *transplant*.

Your kidneys contain a structure called the *glomerulus*, which is responsible for cleansing your blood. Each kidney has hundreds of thousands of glomeruli. Your blood passes through the tiny glomerular capillaries, which are in intimate contact with tubules through which your filtered blood travels. As the filtered blood passes through the tubules, most of the water and the normal contents of the blood are reabsorbed and sent back into your body, while a small amount of water and waste passes from the kidney into the ureter and then into the bladder and out through the urethra.

Progressive changes

Kidney damage caused by diabetic nephropathy progresses through three stages and reversing the damage is possible if you catch it early. The stages are as follows:

  ✔ Very early on, a characteristic called *microalbuminuria* can be detected in the urine. If you've just been diagnosed with type 2 diabetes, your doctor must check for microalbuminuria. If test results are negative, your urine should be checked annually. When microalbuminuria is found, it's still early enough to reverse any damage. A second positive test should lead to preventive action to protect the kidneys, and your doctor should devise an appropriate treatment program (see the following section).

✔ After five years of poorly controlled diabetes, significant expansion of the *mesangial tissue*, the cells between the glomeruler capillaries, occurs. The amount of microalbuminuria is very consistent with the amount of mesangial expansion.

✔ Over the next 15 to 20 years, the open capillaries and tubules are squeezed shut by the encroaching tissues and appear like round nodules (known as *Kimmelstiel-Wilson nodules*, after the names of their discoverers). These nodules are diagnostic of diabetic nephropathy. As the glomeruli are replaced by nodules, less and less filtration of the blood can take place. The blood urea nitrogen begins to rise, ultimately ending in *uraemia* when the kidneys aren't doing any cleansing.

Other factors that contribute to the continuing destruction of the kidneys include abnormal blood fats, cigarette smoking, genetic inheritance and high blood pressure (refer to the section 'Measuring Blood Pressure' earlier in the chapter).

Getting treatment

Happily, you can avoid all the inconvenience and discomfort associated with diabetic nephropathy.

The following are a few key treatments that your doctor can prescribe to prevent the disease or significantly slow it down once it begins:

✔ **Control your blood glucose:** Tightly controlling your blood glucose helps to reverse the damaging process. (For information on controlling your blood glucose, see Part III.)

✔ **Control your blood pressure:** Good control of your blood pressure protects your kidneys from rapid deterioration. Treatment begins with a low-salt diet, but drugs are usually needed. (See Chapter 7 for more information on blood pressure drugs.)

✓ **Control the blood fats:** It's important to lower triglycerides and LDL cholesterol and raise HDL cholesterol (refer to the section 'Tracking Cholesterol and Other Fats' earlier in this chapter). A number of excellent drugs can do this (see Chapter 7).

✓ **Avoid other damage to the kidneys:** Treat urinary tract infections to avoid kidney damage but don't use non-steroidal anti-inflammatory agents (NSAIDS), which can damage the kidneys. Intravenous dyes (or contrast) used in some X-ray procedures or angiograms can also damage the kidneys and special precautions may need to be taken if you need to have one of these tests.

✓ **Conduct dialysis if preventive treatment fails:** Two dialysis techniques are in use at the time of writing:

- **Haemodialysis** is usually done in a hospital and the patient's artery is hooked into a tube that runs through a filtering machine that cleanses the blood and then sends it back into the patient's bloodstream.

- **Peritoneal dialysis** is usually done at home and a tube is inserted into the body cavity that contains the stomach, liver and intestines, called the *peritoneal cavity*. A large quantity of fluid is dripped into the cavity, and it draws out the wastes, which are then removed as the fluid drains out of the cavity.

✓ **Receive a kidney transplant if preventive treatment fails:** While patients who receive a kidney transplant do seem to do better than dialysis patients, most patients stay on dialysis because of the lack of donor kidneys in Australia. Patients who receive a donor kidney must take anti-rejection drugs because the body can reject the foreign organ.

Having a Look at Eye Disease

The eyes are the second major organ of the body affected by diabetes over the long term. While some eye diseases, such as glaucoma and cataracts, also occur in people without diabetes, they appear at a higher rate and earlier in people with diabetes. Glaucoma and cataracts respond to treatment very well. Diabetic retinopathy, however, is limited to those with diabetes and may lead to blindness. In the past, blindness was inevitable, but this outcome is far from the case today.

The following eye diseases are commonly found in people with diabetes:

- **Cataracts:** Cataracts are opaque areas of the lens that can block vision if they're large enough. Cataracts can be surgically removed by a fairly routine operation. The entire lens is removed, and an artificial lens is put in its place. With removal, you have an excellent chance for the restoration of your vision.

- **Glaucoma:** High pressure inside the eye is enough to do damage to the optic nerve. Fortunately, medical treatment can lower the eye pressure and save the eye. Optometrists and eye doctors check for glaucoma on a routine basis.

- **Retinopathy:** Diabetic retinopathy refers to a number of changes that are seen on the retina of the eye. While no drugs are available at the time of writing to treat retinopathy, laser and other types of surgery can help to treat it. The two types of retinopathy are

  - **Background retinopathy:** This type of retinopathy can be a predictor of worse problems. The first changes noted by the ophthalmologist are small haemorrhages or *retinal aneurysms*, which are the result of weakening of the capillaries of the eye with production of outpocketing of the capillaries.

  - **Proliferative retinopathy:** This type of retinopathy ends in loss of vision if untreated. Just as in many other parts of the body when the blood supply is reduced, new blood vessels form to carry more blood to the retina. When this happens, the patient is entering the stage of proliferative retinopathy.

You must get an annual eye examination by an optometrist or ophthalmologist (a specialist eye doctor) to preserve your vision. All kinds of procedures can be done if abnormalities are found, but they must be discovered first. Get an eye examination as soon as you're diagnosed with type 2 diabetes and every year after that.

Reining in Neuropathy, or Nerve Disease

The third major organ system of the body that's attacked by poorly controlled diabetes is the nervous system. Forty per cent of people with diabetes have some abnormality of the nervous system but usually don't realise it because this condition doesn't have any early symptoms. These people usually have poor glucose control, smoke and are over 40 years of age. Nerve disease is found most often in those who've had diabetes the longest. The major problem with respect to diabetic neuropathy is the high incidence of foot infections, foot ulcerations and amputations (covered in the section 'Fabulous Feet', later in the chapter).

How high glucose levels damage nerves remains uncertain. What is found is that the part of the nerve, called the *axon*, that connects to other nerves, or to muscle, degenerates. Researchers believe that the damage is due to a cut-off in the blood supply to the nerve (vascular) in some cases, and to chemical toxins produced by the metabolism of too much glucose (metabolic) in others.

Diabetic neuropathy occurs in any situation where the blood glucose is abnormally elevated for extended periods of time. When the elevated blood glucose is brought down to normal levels, the signs and symptoms improve. In some cases, the neuropathy disappears.

The fact that intensive control of the blood glucose improves the neuropathy suggests that it's a consequence of abnormal metabolism that damages the nerves.

Diagnosing neuropathy

The speed with which a nervous impulse travels down a nerve fibre is called the *nerve conduction velocity*. In diabetic neuropathy, the nerve conduction velocity (NCV) is slowed. In addition to persistently high blood glucose levels, neuropathy is made worse in the following circumstances:

- ✔ **Age:** Neuropathy is most common over the age of 40.
- ✔ **Alcohol consumption:** Even small quantities of alcohol can make neuropathy worse.
- ✔ **Height:** Neuropathy is more common in taller individuals, who have longer nerve fibres to damage.

Doctors can test nerve function in a variety of ways because different nerve fibres seem to be responsible for different kinds of sensation, such as light touch, temperature and vibration. The connection between the kind of test and the fibre it tests for is as follows:

- ✔ **Light touch testing**, perhaps the most important test performed, tests the large fibres, which sense anything touching our skin.

- ✔ **Temperature testing**, using a warm or cold item, tests for damage to small fibres, which prevent you burning yourself by touching something hot.

- ✔ **Vibration testing**, using a tuning fork or a machine called a *biothesiometer*, brings out abnormalities of large nerve fibres.

Symptoms of neuropathy

The various disorders of the nervous system are broken down into three categories of disorders: Loss of sensation, loss of automatic (known as *autonomic*) nerves and loss of motor nerves. The following describes these in more detail:

- ✔ **Disorders of sensation:** The most common and bothersome disorders of nerves in diabetes. A number of different conditions occur, including

  - • **Peripheral neuropathy:** Generally presenting itself in the feet and hands, people notice a diminished (or increased) sense of touch, pain or temperature, or the sensation of tingling or burning. The symptoms are often worse at night. The danger is that if people can't feel their feet properly, they don't know, without looking down, whether they have trauma to their foot, such as a burn or an injury from stepping on a piece of glass. This condition can lead to the neuropathic foot ulcer (see the section 'Fabulous Feet' later in this chapter).

  - • **Diabetic amyotrophy:** A mixture of pain and loss of muscle strength in the muscles of the upper leg, this results in the person not being able to straighten the knee, and pain extending down from the hip to the thigh. Generally runs a short course, but may continue for years.

  - • **Radiculopathy-nerve root involvement:** A severe pain distributed in a horizontal line around one side of the chest or abdomen, suggesting damage to the root of the nerve as it leaves the spinal column. Pain usually goes away after 6 to 24 months.

✓ **Disorders of automatic (autonomic) nerves:** These disorders affect the muscles, such as the heart, diaphragm, oesophagus, stomach and intestines, that are moving all the time without you having to think about it. Depending upon the nerve involved, disorders of the autonomic nerves include

- Bladder abnormalities, starting with a loss of the sensation of bladder fullness.

- Sexual dysfunction in 50 per cent of males (impotence) with diabetes and 30 per cent of females with diabetes.

- Intestinal abnormalities of various kinds.

- Involvement of the large intestine that can result in diabetic diarrhoea with as many as ten or more bowel movements in a day.

- Heart abnormalities from loss of nerves to the heart.

- Sweating problems, especially in the feet.

- Abnormalities of the pupil of the eye.

✓ **Disorders of movement:** In this disorder, nerves to the muscles are affected, causing a sudden inability to move or use the muscles. For example, if the nerve to the face is affected, the eyelid may droop or the smile on one side of the face may be flat. The patient can have trouble with vision or problems with hearing. The disorder goes away of its own accord after several months.

For more information on the above disorders and their treatments, refer to *Diabetes For Dummies, 3rd Australian Edition*.

You can see that you can run into all kinds of problems if you develop diabetic neuropathy. None of them need ever bother you, though, if you follow the recommendations in Part III.

Fabulous Feet

People with diabetes are prone to a range of foot problems due to peripheral neuropathy and peripheral vascular disease, which can cause numbness, burning and tingling, ulcers and very occasionally amputation.

The good news, however, is that diabetic feet can be fabulous. This result just takes a little more care — from you and from your diabetes care team. The information below covers common foot problems and how you can prevent them, assessing your feet for these problems and how you can treat them if they do arise.

Caring for your feet — prevention is better than cure

The key to fabulous feet — and successful long-term foot care — is prevention. The following is a list of ways to help you put your best foot forward and stop foot problems occurring in the first place:

✔ **Book a foot assessment:** Soon after you've been diagnosed with type 2 diabetes, see your doctor or podiatrist for an assessment of your feet to check blood supply and nerve function. Your podiatrist can also advise you on choosing appropriate shoes and direct you to specialist shops that understand the needs of people with diabetes.

✔ **Check your feet:** Check your feet every day, including the sole of the foot and between the toes. Look for anything that's abnormal or wasn't present the previous day. If you find a problem, do something about it immediately and if you can see no improvement in a problem area on your foot after 24 to 48 hours, or the wound becomes red and hot, see your GP or podiatrist.

If you find it difficult to see under your feet, use a mirror. Ask someone to look at your feet for you if you can't see properly.

✔ **Look after your skin:** Perform a daily care routine where you wash your feet in warm water with a mild soap and dry your feet carefully. If the skin between your toes becomes white and soggy, apply a small amount of methylated spirits using a cotton bud. If the condition doesn't improve, see your GP. Apply a urea-based moisturising cream twice daily to help prevent the skin getting too dry.

✔ **Look after your toe nails:** If you can cut your own nails, cut them straight across and not too short. Check afterwards to ensure you haven't left any sharp edges; if sharp edges are present, use a nail file to smooth them. See a podiatrist to cut your nails if you have problems reaching or seeing your feet, or your nails are thickened or otherwise abnormal.

✔ **Wear the right shoes:** Prevention of ulcers and infection starts with having well-fitted, appropriate footwear, and wearing this footwear all the time — not just to the diabetes clinic or podiatrist. Good shoes aren't cheap, but they're an important investment in your health.

✔ **Wear the right socks:** Choose socks made from cotton or natural fibres. Moisture can build up inside synthetic fibre socks.

The Australian government subsidises a number of visits to a podiatrist per year for people with diabetes. Your GP can organise this.

Identifying common foot problems

All feet are prone to problems such as bunions and corns, especially if you wear ill-fitting shoes. However, these problems can become much more serious if you have diabetes. Here's a list of some common problems:

✔ **Dry, cracked skin:** People with diabetes are prone to dry, cracked skin as a result of nerve damage. Not only does this feel uncomfortable and itchy, but cracks in the skin also allow bacteria to get in and cause infection.

✔ **Calluses and corns:** High-heeled, long, narrow shoes may look gorgeous but can result in areas of thickened skin at sites of pressure, known as calluses or corns. For people with diabetes, this area can become a potential site for ulceration.

✔ **Diabetic foot ulcers:** Diabetic foot ulcers can be a major problem for people with diabetes, mainly due to a lack of feeling in the feet and poor circulation. If your feet feel numb, you can injure your feet without being aware of it — for example, you could stand on a sharp stone or cut your foot and be totally unaware that you've done so. You could walk around with a pebble in your shoe for a week without feeling it. A foot ulcer can develop from a minor injury to the foot — and if you have limited vision or mobility, you may not be able to see the ulcer, allowing it to progress.

✔ **Foot infections:** If you have diabetes, you generally have a higher risk of bacterial or fungal infections. In Australia's mostly hot and often humid climate, fungal infections of the foot and between the toes are common. Bacterial infections may occur more easily if the skin is dry and cracked. Any of these infections can cause more serious complications in people with diabetes, such as ulcers or even amputation.

✔ **Foot deformity:** Diabetes can also affect motor nerves that supply leg muscles (refer to the section 'Reining in Neuropathy, or Nerve Disease' earlier in this chapter). Nerve damage can lead to a condition of the toes called 'clawing' and the loss of the arch in the foot. This redistributes the load on the foot, making walking more unbalanced. This unbalanced gait puts excessive pressure on certain parts of the sole of the foot, which can cause ulceration.

For more information about common foot problems and their treatments, refer to *Diabetes For Dummies, 3rd Australian Edition*.

Treating foot problems

Despite your best efforts, problems with your feet may develop that require medication or surgery.

The pain associated with peripheral sensory neuropathy (which may include intense tingling in the feet or pins and needles, which often gets worse at night) is sometimes treated with drugs that include amitriptyline (also used as an antidepressant) or gabapentin (also used as an anticonvulsant). As with all medications, risks and benefits exist with these drugs, so remember to ask your GP or diabetes specialist about these.

Bacterial infections may complicate ulcers and require antibiotics. Infections involving the bone require higher doses of antibiotics and a prolonged course of treatment; intravenous antibiotics are usually required in this situation. Fungal infections of the foot and toenails, such as tinea, are very common for people with diabetes, and these infections often require prolonged topical or oral anti-fungal agents.

If you have a foot infection, always see your GP to confirm the diagnosis rather than treating it yourself.

Doctors try to avoid surgery if possible, because losing a toe (or more) can be very psychologically distressing, a period of recovery is required and the loss of a toe can change the biomechanics of the foot in such a way that walking becomes more difficult and remaining toes can start to claw.

Sexual Problems in Diabetes

Diabetes can cause problems with sexual functioning for both men and women. However, with the proper treatment, you can enjoy a rewarding sex life.

Male sexual problems

If carefully questioned, up to 50 per cent of all males with diabetes admit to some difficulty with sexual function. This difficulty usually takes the form of *erectile dysfunction*, the inability to have or sustain an erection sufficient for intercourse. Many factors besides diabetes cause this problem, and you should rule them out before blaming diabetes. Some other possibilities include the following:

- Hormonal abnormalities, such as insufficient production of the male hormone testosterone or overproduction of a hormone from the pituitary gland, called *prolactin*
- Injury to the penis
- Medications such as some antihypertensives and antidepressants
- Poor blood supply to the penis due to blockage of the artery by peripheral vascular disease, which can be treated very effectively by microvascular surgery
- *Psychogenic impotence*, an inability to have an erection for psychological rather than physical reasons
- Other vascular risk factors including hypertension, obesity, known cardiovascular disease and smoking

After you eliminate all the other possibilities for erectile dysfunction, diabetes is then considered to be the source of the problem. In order for you to understand how diabetes affects an erection, we briefly describe how an erection is normally achieved, before discussing how erectile dysfunction caused by diabetes can be treated.

Impeding the erection process

Diabetes can damage the parasympathetic nervous system so that the male can't get an erection sufficient for sexual intercourse. The sympathetic nervous system is spared, so that ejaculation and orgasm can occur. Of course, intercourse may be unpleasant for the partners because of the consequences of the inability of the male to achieve a firm erection.

Keep in mind that other factors can also play a role. The duration of your diabetes, your control over blood glucose, drugs, alcohol and state of mind can all play a role in erection failure.

Treating erectile dysfunction

Fortunately for the male with diabetes and with erectile dysfunction, numerous approaches to treatment exist, beginning with drugs, continuing with external devices to create an erection, and ending with implantable devices that provide a very satisfactory erection. Treatment is successful in between 70 and 80 per cent of men, but only a small percentage ever discuss the problem with their doctor.

Treatment options for erectile dysfunction include the following:

✔ **Oral tablets such as Viagra, Levitra or Cialis:** These medications belong to the same class of drug called phosphodiesterase inhibitors. They work by relaxing the blood vessels in the penis when a man becomes sexually aroused. Possible side effects include headaches, light-headedness, dizziness, distorted vision, facial flushing or indigestion.

Men who taking nitrate drugs (usually used for chest pain) should not take Viagra. The combination of Viagra and nitrates may cause a significant and possibly fatal drop in blood pressure.

✔ **Injection into the penis:** You can inject alprostadil (marketed as Caverject) directly into the penis to create an erection. Alprostadil is a chemical that relaxes the blood vessels in the penis to allow more flow, and doesn't require sexual stimulation in order to work. Complications of injections are rare but include bruising, pain and the formation of nodules at the injection site.

A very rare complication of injecting alprostadil into the penis is *priapism*, where the penis maintains its erection for many hours. If the erection lasts for more than four hours, you must see your doctor.

> ✓ **Vacuum constriction devices:** These tubes, which fit over the penis, create a closed space when pressed against the patient's body. A pump draws out the air in the tube, and blood rushes into the penis to replace the air. Once the penis is erect, a rubber band is placed around the base of the penis to keep the blood inside it. The rubber band may be kept on for up to 30 minutes.

> ✓ **Implanted penile prostheses:** A *prosthesis* (an artificial substitute) can be implanted in the penis to give a very satisfactory erection. An inflatable prosthesis involves a pump in the scrotal sac that contains fluid. The pump can be squeezed to transfer the fluid into balloons in the penis to stiffen it. When not pumped up, the penis appears normally soft.

Female sexual problems

Because the female doesn't have a penis that must enlarge for sex, the sexual complications of diabetes aren't as visually obvious. However, the problems can be just as difficult for women. Menopause must be ruled out first because a dry vagina and irregular menstrual function are also symptoms of menopause.

The following problems are associated with diabetes:

> ✓ A dry mouth and vagina because of high blood glucose.

> ✓ Irregular menstrual cycles when your diabetes isn't well controlled or you gain or lose a lot of weight.

> ✓ Yeast infections (such as thrush) of the vagina.

> ✓ Feeling unattractive due to being overweight.

> ✓ Loss of bladder control due to a neurogenic bladder.

The female with long-standing diabetes may have several other problems that are specific to her sexual organs. These problems include reduced lubrication because of parasympathetic nerve involvement, reduced blood flow because of diabetic blood vessel disease and loss of skin sensation around the vaginal area.

Most women who have problems with lubrication use over-the-counter preparations to lubricate themselves. The lubrication product you use is a matter of choice, although water-based products, like K-Y jelly, are probably the easiest to use and clean up, and the safest if using condoms. Petroleum-based lubricants are not recommended because of the possibility of bacterial infection.

Oestrogen, which can be taken by mouth or placed in the dry vagina in pessary form, also may be useful for the post-menopausal woman. Talk to your GP or gynaecologist about finding the right combination of treatments to suit you.

Skin Disease in Diabetes

Many conditions involve the skin and are unique to the person with diabetes because of the treatment and complications of the disease. The most common complications involving the skin include the following:

- *Acanthosis nigricans*, a velvety-feeling increase in pigmentation on the back of the neck and the armpits, causes no medical problems and needs no specific treatment. This condition is usually found when *hyperinsulinaemia* (excessive amounts of insulin) and insulin resistance are present, and is also seen in children with type 2 diabetes.

- Diabetic thick skin, which is thicker than normal skin, occurs in people who have had diabetes for more than ten years. This includes Dupuytren's contractures, where fascia under the skin of the palms can thicken and cause contraction of the skin. This can affect the hand tendons, which can be corrected with surgery.

- Fungal infections occur under the nails or between the toes. Fungus likes moisture and elevated glucose. Medications may cure this problem, but it recurs if glucose and moisture aren't managed.

- *Insulin hypertrophy* (fat hypertrophy) is the accumulation of fatty tissue where insulin is injected. This normal action of insulin is prevented by moving the injection site around.

- *Xanthelasma*, which are small yellow flat areas called plaques on the eyelids, occur even when cholesterol is not elevated.

Part III

Living with Type 2 Diabetes: Your Physical Health

Glenn Lumsden

*'If Bob has diabetes, how come he looks
so much fitter than us?'*

In this part ...

1 s it possible that you could be healthier with type 2 diabetes than your friends who don't have diabetes? This part shows that the answer to that question is yes. While others without diabetes, who may not be aware they even have any health problems, are left to their own devices, you can find out exactly what you have to do — not just to live with diabetes, but to thrive with diabetes. The steps you need to take are simple and basic — they just require a little effort. In no time, however, you'll probably be asking yourself, 'Why didn't I think of that?'

Chapter 6

Glucose Monitoring and Other Tests

· ·

In This Chapter

▶ Understanding the importance of using testing to manage your diabetes

▶ Checking your blood glucose levels

▶ Choosing a blood glucose meter

▶ Checking glycosylated haemoglobin (HbA1c)

· ·

*I*f you read Part II, you know all about the complications that can happen to you if you have diabetes. In the next four chapters (Part III), we discuss the options you can adopt to help you avoid these complications and manage your diabetes. Things are improving all the time — most of the products and treatments covered in this part weren't available 20 years ago, and some of the new products now available can have a dramatic effect on how well you manage your diabetes. While you may think it's a bit of an inconvenience and an expense, your health is worth it.

Part II wasn't intended to worry you, but to set out clearly just what having diabetes can involve. In this chapter, you discover all you need to know to put your diabetes in its proper place. You find out how well you're currently controlling your blood glucose and what changes you may need to make in your treatment to ensure your target blood glucose levels are met.

Testing, Testing: Tests You Need to Stay Healthy

How are doctors actually doing in medical care for a person with diabetes? In Sydney, staff at the St Vincent's Hospital Diabetes Centre looked at whether standard tests that should be performed regularly on patients with diabetes had been completed. Staff documented whether glycosylated haemoglobin (HbA1c) had been checked, whether an annual dilated eye examination (which can be done by your optometrist) had been completed, whether blood pressure and lipids (blood fats) had been measured recently and whether kidney and nerve function had also been reviewed. Staff also checked whether the diabetes educator and dietitian services provided were used appropriately. See the section 'Tracking Your Glucose Over Time with Glycosylated Haemoglobin' later in this chapter for more.

The results revealed the following:

- Almost two-thirds of the centre's patients had the majority of these tests completed on a regular basis.

- One-third of the people had seen a diabetes educator and less than one-fifth had seen a dietitian in the previous two years.

- More than half of those with type 1 diabetes were achieving an HbA1c of less than 8 per cent and two-thirds of those with type 2 diabetes were also meeting this target. (See the section 'Tracking Your Glucose over Time with Glycosylated Haemoglobin' for more on target levels.)

- About half of the centre's patients with type 1 diabetes and about one-third of patients with type 2 diabetes were achieving recommended blood pressure goals.

- Half the patients were achieving the targets for blood fats.

Obviously, doctors and members of diabetes care teams can still do more to ensure all patients are tested appropriately and that more people achieve their target health goals; however, these results also reflect a need for people with diabetes to be more aware of what's required to manage their condition. Knowing what's required means you can monitor your own management of diabetes — and remind your doctors as needed! This chapter provides everything you need to know.

Monitoring Your Blood Glucose

Insulin was extracted and used for the first time more than 80 years ago. Since then, nothing has improved the life of people with diabetes as much as the ability to measure their own blood glucose with a drop of blood. Prior to blood glucose self-monitoring, testing the urine for glucose was the only way to determine whether blood glucose was high, but urine testing couldn't tell at all whether the glucose was low. The urine test for glucose is, therefore, worthless for controlling blood glucose, although testing the urine for other things such as ketones and protein can be of value.

Understanding the technology is simple enough. The glucose in a drop of your blood reacts with an enzyme on a special test strip. The reaction produces electrons, and a meter (electronic) then converts the amount of electrons into a glucose reading. Each meter (glucometer) has its own corresponding test strip. They aren't interchangeable!

One of the first things that was learnt when blood glucose self-testing became available is that a person with diabetes, even someone whose condition is fairly stable, can have tremendous variation in glucose levels, especially in association with food, but even in the fasting state before breakfast. This is why multiple tests are needed throughout the day.

How often should you test?

How often you test is determined by the kind of treatment you're using to control your type 2 diabetes, and the level of stability of your blood glucose levels, as follows:

- ✔ **If you're on insulin, you need to test three to four times per day.** Remember to vary the times so you test both before and after meals. Testing at these times helps you to assess whether the treatment and doses you're on are the most appropriate.

- ✔ **If you're on tablets, you need to test twice per day.** Testing twice per day at varying times helps you measure the effect of the treatment. If your glucose levels are consistently stable — between 4 and 8 mmol/L over several weeks or one month — you may only need to test once per day, alternating between pre- and two hours post-meals. Testing in this manner can be enough to keep you aware of your diabetes control.

- ✔ **If you're managing type 2 diabetes just through diet and exercise, you don't need to test.** If you're able to manage your diabetes with just diet and exercise, you shouldn't need to frequently monitor your blood glucose levels — but always check what your GP or diabetes educator advises. You still need to have a glycosylated haemoglobin test every four to six months to ensure your glucose levels continue to be stable. (See the section 'Tracking Your Glucose over Time with Glycosylated Haemoglobin' later in this chapter for more on this test.)

- ✔ **If you're pregnant, you need to test more often.** Expectant mothers with diabetes are encouraged to test between six and seven times per day in order to keep their developing foetus as healthy as possible.

Blood glucose testing can be useful in showing you how the things you do through the day affect your blood glucose levels. If you eat something not normally part of your diet and want to test its effect on your glucose, do a test. If you're about to exercise, a blood glucose test can tell you whether you need to eat before starting the exercise or whether you can use the exercise to bring your glucose down.

How do you perform the test?

If you don't already have a meter, the next section on choosing one is essential reading. Performing a blood glucose test is quite straightforward — while all blood glucose meters work a little differently, all meters require a drop of blood, usually from the finger. To get a drop of blood, you can use a finger-prick lancet, either on its own or contained within an automatic device. Many automatic devices are spring-loaded so you push a button and the lancet springs out and pricks your finger. Some glucose meters come with their own recommended finger-prick devices.

To perform a blood glucose test, you need the following:

- ✔ Blood glucose meter
- ✔ Blood glucose record book
- ✔ Cotton wool ball or tissue
- ✔ Disposable test strip
- ✔ Lancet device

Your meter has an in-built memory, so make sure the correct date and time are set on it. That way, you can look back at the reading and know whether it was taken in the early morning or late at night! Some meters allow you to download these readings onto a computer, so you can print out the results and take them with you when you see your doctor or diabetes educator.

 Keep a blood glucose record book where you can write down each of your readings, even if your meter has a memory. Writing down the results enables you to reflect on your glucose levels at different times of the day and to see the effect different foods or activities have on your glucose level. You can then discuss these different situations with your doctor, diabetes educator and/or dietitian. Record books are available from your local diabetes centre or the Australian Diabetes Council (in NSW) or Diabetes Australia in other states and territories.

Keep the following in mind when you're testing your glucose:

- ✔ **Wash your hands with soap and warm water and dry thoroughly.**

- ✔ **If you have trouble getting blood, warm up your hand.** Rub your hands together or put them under warm water.

- ✔ **If your meter requires a code, make sure that the code for the strips matches the code in the meter.**

- ✔ **Prepare the lancing device by inserting a fresh lancet.** Lancets that are used more than once are not as sharp as a new lancet, and can cause more pain and injury to the skin.

- ✔ **Discard any unused strips in the vial after 90 days because the test strips may deteriorate.** Studies have shown that the qualities of test strips that are loose in a vial deteriorate rapidly if the vial is left open. Two hours of exposure to air may ruin the strips, so be sure to replace the cap on the vial. Strips that are individually foil-wrapped don't have this problem.

- ✔ **Don't let others use your meter.** The test results of others will be mixed in with your tests if they're downloaded into a computer or if your GP or diabetes care team go back through the meter's memory to see what's been happening.

 Light, moisture and heat can all adversely affect the test strips. Ensure the lid is tightly fastened after use, you store the strips in a cool, dry place (not the refrigerator!) and you keep the desiccant (usually a small, white packet) in the bottle.

Investigating Blood Glucose Meters

So many meters are on the market that you may be confused about which one to use. One consideration that should play no part in your decision is its cost; some manufacturers are happy to give you the meter because you're then required to purchase their test strips. Each manufacturer makes a different test strip, and they're not interchangeable with other machines. The cost of blood glucose meters has dropped dramatically over the years and a reliable meter costs less than $50.

Because the meters are so cheap and the science is changing so rapidly, get a new meter every year or two to make sure that you have the latest, state of the art, device. The cost of test strips is the same from meter to meter, so their cost doesn't have to play a big role in your meter decision, either.

Another aspect that you need not be concerned about is the accuracy of the various machines. All are accurate to a degree acceptable for managing your diabetes. Keep in mind, though, that they don't have the accuracy of a laboratory. They're probably different by about 10 per cent (above or below) compared to what can be achieved in a laboratory.

So how do you choose the right meter for you? Well, doctors sometimes have meters that they prefer to work with because a computer program can download the test results from the meter and display them in a certain way. This analysis can be enormously helpful in deciding how to adjust your treatment for the best control of your glucose, but it's not essential.

To satisfy yourself that you have the right meter for your purposes, ask the following questions when choosing a meter:

- Does the manufacturer provide a readily available and reliable back-up service?

- If a meter is manufactured overseas, is servicing for it available in Australia and is the warranty valid here? And are the results produced by the meter measured in mmol/L?

✔ Are the batteries readily available or are they hard to get and expensive?

✔ Does the meter have a memory that you or your doctor can check?

✔ Is the data stored on the meter downloadable to a computer program that can manipulate the data?

✔ How quickly does the meter display the results? Some meters can display results in as little as five seconds.

✔ Is the meter suitable if you're pregnant or planning a pregnancy?

✔ Is the meter suitable for the types of other medications that you might be taking? If you require peritoneal dialysis, for example, this need affects the type of meter you require.

The National Diabetes Services Scheme (NDSS) is funded by the Commonwealth government and offers subsidised test strips to its registered members, so make sure you sign up. If you have private health insurance, your fund may also offer some rebate on a meter if you purchase it, so check with your health fund before you buy.

Talk to your diabetes educator about choosing a blood glucose meter that's right for you. She can cut down the confusion between meters and make the choice simpler. Choose the meter you like, not necessarily the one the doctor likes!

Tracking Your Glucose over Time with Glycosylated Haemoglobin

Individual blood glucose tests are great for deciding how you're doing at one particular moment and what to do to make improvements, but they don't give the big picture — they're just a moment in time. Glucose can change a great deal even in an hour. What's needed is a test that gives an overall picture of blood glucose levels over many days, weeks or even months. The test that accomplishes this important task is called a glycosylated haemoglobin (HbA1c) test.

Understanding how a HbA1c works

Haemoglobin is a protein that carries oxygen around the body and drops it off wherever it's needed to help in all the chemical reactions that are constantly taking place. The haemoglobin is packaged within red blood cells and it's what gives these cells their colour. Red blood cells live in the bloodstream for between 60 and 90 days.

Glucose attaches in several different ways to the haemoglobin and the total of all the haemoglobin attached to glucose is called *glycohaemoglobin* or *glycosylated haemoglobin*. Once red blood cells become attached to glucose, they stay attached until they die (the cells live for up to three months). As red blood cells die, new ones are produced and glucose can again attach itself to these new cells. The largest proportion of total glycosylated haemoglobin, and therefore the easiest to measure, is known as HbA1c.

The HbA1c test counts the amount of glucose attached to the red blood cells and reports it as a percentage. For example, if 7 out of every 100 red blood cells have glucose attached, the HbA1c result will be 7 per cent. Because glycosylated haemoglobin remains in the blood for up to three months, testing HbA1c levels is a reflection of the glucose control over that whole period.

Blood glucose tests measure the amount of glucose freely circulating in the blood at that given moment, so they use a different unit of measure to the HbA1c test. Blood glucose tests measure millimoles of glucose per litre of blood — or mmol/L. A HbA1c isn't an average of blood glucose levels, but consistently high blood glucose levels will result in more glycosylated red blood cells, thereby increasing HbA1c.

Figure 6-1 shows you the correlation between the HbA1c and blood glucose: A HbA1c of less than 6 per cent corresponds to an average blood glucose of less than 6.6 mmol/L, while a HbA1c of 7 per cent reflects an average blood glucose of 8.3 mmol/L.

Another test similar to HbA1c is *fructosamine*. This test measures blood glucose levels combined with protein in the blood, and reflects the level of blood glucose for the past three weeks. The test can prove to be very useful when you need to know the effect of a treatment change very rapidly — as is the case for pregnant women with gestational diabetes, for example.

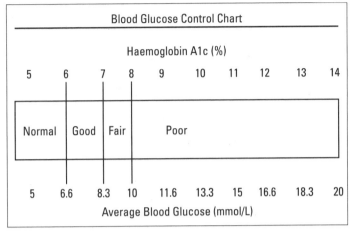

Figure 6-1: Comparison between HbA1c and blood glucose.

Looking at factors that affect HbA1c results

To be accurate, the HbA1c test relies on a three-month lifespan of red blood cells, and this lifespan can sometimes be altered, affecting the HbA1c results. Circumstances that can affect the lifespan of the red blood cells include the following:

- ✔ Any illness that affects red blood cell survival
- ✔ Blood transfusion (including blood donation)
- ✔ Kidney failure

Unfortunately, not all laboratories conduct the HbA1c test in the same way and this can affect your result. You need to know the normal value in the lab where you had the test. Fortunately, each lab usually has a column on its result form showing the normal values for each test. Still, it makes for a lot of confusion.

Have your HbA1c measured in the same laboratory each time, so that levels can be tracked across the year. This avoids the problem of getting results from different testing methods between laboratories.

Acting on a HbA1c result

Studies have shown that normal HbA1c levels — that is, in people without diabetes — are between 4 and 6 per cent. (Check with the lab where your test is processed for its normal values, and remember that variation can occur within the given normal ranges.)

The Royal Australian College of General Practitioners and Diabetes Australia recommend taking action to control the blood glucose if the HbA1c is 7 per cent or greater. Further monitoring and investigation is required between 6 and 7 per cent; the goal is to achieve less than or equal to 7 per cent.

If you have type 2 diabetes, your doctor should test you four times a year for HbA1c. A good HbA1c result is highly motivating to keep up good self-care, while a poor result immediately tells you that you need tighter control.

Chapter 7

Medications: What You Should Know

. . . .

In This Chapter

▶ Reviewing drugs taken orally

▶ Looking at injecting drugs to help treat type 2 diabetes

▶ Finding out about insulin

▶ Understanding other drugs often prescribed to people with diabetes

▶ Steering clear of dangerous drug combinations

▶ Getting financial assistance with the cost of medication

. . . .

*Y*ou need to take medication if diet and exercise aren't keeping your blood glucose under control. (See Chapters 8 and 9 for tips on using diet and exercise to manage your diabetes.) The good news is that since 1921, when insulin was isolated and used for the first time, and the 1950s, when the first oral medications for type 2 diabetes became available, new classes of drugs have been developed, each lowering blood glucose in its own unique way.

In this chapter, you become an educated consumer, finding out all you need to know to use medication effectively and safely. You can find out not only about the medication you're taking and how it works, but also when to take it, how it interacts with other medications and what side effects it may cause. We also advise you on how to use several of these medications together, if necessary, to normalise your blood glucose.

Taking Drugs by Mouth: Oral Agents

Most people with type 2 diabetes start off taking tablets to help control their blood glucose. In the following sections, we discuss the various oral medications prescribed to help manage diabetes.

No drug should be taken as a convenient way of avoiding the basic diet and exercise practices that are the keys to good control (see Chapters 8 and 9 for information about these crucial factors).

Metformin

As recommended by The Royal Australian College of General Practitioners and Diabetes Australia, Metformin is usually the first medication prescribed for most people with type 2 diabetes. It's available in 500-milligram, 850-milligram and 1,000-milligram (1-gram) strengths. Brand names include Diabex, Diaformin, Formet, Glucohexal, Glucomet and Glucophage.

The starting dose for metformin is usually 500 milligrams one to three times daily, and the maximum dose is usually 3 grams per day, taken in two to three doses with meals. However, a new controlled-release preparation of metformin is now available (marketed as Diabex XR or Diaformin XR). These preparations come in 500-milligram and 1,000-milligram tablets and only need to be taken once per day. The maximum dose for the controlled-release preparation is 2 grams per day. If blood glucose isn't adequately controlled, a second tablet is usually added; which drug is chosen depends on your individual circumstances.

The characteristics of metformin are that it

- ✔ Lowers blood glucose, mainly by reducing the production of glucose from the liver (hepatic glucose output) and increasing insulin sensitivity; it may slow the uptake of glucose from the intestine.

- ✔ Can cause nausea and diarrhoea; this can be reduced by taking the tablet with food, starting at a low dose and increasing slowly.

- ✔ Might take a couple of weeks to be effective.

✔ Doesn't, by itself (monotherapy), cause hypoglycaemia. When given in combination with a sulphonylurea (see following section), can cause hypoglycaemia; if persistent, the dose of sulphonylurea is reduced.

✔ Is removed from the body by the kidneys; if the kidneys aren't working well, the dose of metformin needs to be reduced.

✔ Doesn't depend on stimulating insulin to work, unlike sulphonylureas.

✔ Is often associated with weight loss, possibly from the gastrointestinal irritation or because your stomach can feel more full for longer after a meal.

✔ Shouldn't be used when you have significant liver disease, kidney disease or heart failure.

✔ Is usually stopped for a day or two before surgery or an X-ray series using a dye.

✔ Shouldn't be used by people who drink alcohol excessively, and isn't usually recommended for use in women who are pregnant or breastfeeding.

Metformin can be a very useful drug, especially when *fasting hyperglycaemia* (high blood glucose upon awakening) is present. Metformin has some positive effects on the blood fats, causing a decrease in triglycerides and LDL cholesterol and an increase in HDL cholesterol.

Metformin is also available as a combination drug with other medications to help lower blood glucose. These medications are available in a variety of strengths and can be useful for people stabilised on both drugs by reducing the number of tablets to swallow each day.

Metformin is available in the following combinations:

✔ **Avandamet**, in combination with rosiglitazone

✔ **Glucovance**, in combination with glibenclamide

✔ **Janumet**, in combination with sitagliptin

Sulphonylureas

Scientists discovered sulphonylureas accidentally when it was noticed that soldiers given certain sulphur-containing antibiotics developed symptoms of low blood glucose. Once scientists began to search for the most potent examples of this effect, they came up with several different versions of this drug. The characteristics of sulphonylureas are that they

- ✓ Work by making the pancreas release more insulin
- ✓ Are capable of causing hypoglycaemia and weight gain
- ✓ Should be taken with or immediately before meals
- ✓ Shouldn't be combined with another medication from this group, or be taken by a woman who's pregnant or breastfeeding
- ✓ Can be fairly potent when given in combination with one of the other classes of oral agents

Some of the more common versions of sulphonylureas and their brand names are: Glibenclamide (Daonil and Glimel); gliclazide (Diamicron and Glyade); glimepiride (Amaryl); and glipizide (Melizide and Minidiab).

Acarbose

Acarbose, brand name Glucobay, blocks the action of an enzyme in the gut called *alpha glucosidase*. This enzyme is responsible for breaking down complex carbohydrates into smaller molecules like glucose and fructose so that they can be absorbed. The result is that the rate in the rise of glucose in the bloodstream is slowed after meals. These carbohydrates are eventually broken down by bacteria lower down in the intestine and produce a lot of flatulence, abdominal pain and diarrhoea, which are the major drawbacks of this drug.

The main characteristics of acarbose are

- ✓ The tablets can be swallowed whole at the beginning of a meal or chewed with the first few mouthfuls of food.
- ✓ The recommended starting dose is 50 milligrams once daily with a gradual increase to 50 milligrams three times daily. This dose can be increased to 100 milligrams three times daily after six to eight weeks, depending on the response; the maximum daily dose is 600 milligrams.
- ✓ It doesn't cause hypoglycaemia when used alone but can in combination with sulphonylureas. If hypoglycaemia is persistent, the dose of sulphonylurea is decreased.

  ✔ It doesn't require insulin for its activity.

  ✔ Many people don't like it because of the gastrointestinal side effects.

  ✔ The lowering of glucose and HbA1c (refer to Chapter 6) is modest at most.

Because acarbose acts by blocking the breakdown of complex carbohydrates, hypoglycaemia occurring with acarbose and sulphonylurea combinations must be treated with a preparation of glucose such as Glucojel jellybeans.

Thiazolidinediones (the glitazones)

The glitazones are the first group of drugs for type 2 diabetes that directly target insulin resistance by causing changes within the muscle and fat cells where the insulin resistance occurs. This means that the body doesn't have to make as much insulin to control the blood glucose.

These changes take several weeks to occur and some people may not respond at all. Because they improve insulin resistance, the greatest effect on blood glucose is shown after eating.

Two glitazones are available in Australia (and are only available on the Pharmaceutical Benefits Scheme through an authority script; strict criteria for use have been laid down by the Australian government):

  ✔ **Pioglitazone** (brand name Actos), which also may help your blood fats, has a starting dose of 15 to 30 milligrams once daily; the dose can be increased after six to eight weeks if necessary to a maximum of 45 milligrams daily.

  ✔ **Rosiglitazone** (brand name Avandia) given once or twice per day, with or without food; the recommended starting dose is 4 milligrams per day; this dose can be increased to 8 milligrams per day after six to eight weeks if greater control of blood glucose is required. It's also available as a combination tablet with metformin (marketed as Avandamet) in a number of different combinations of strengths.

The glitazone drugs can, however, have associated problems. They

- ✔ Can cause fluid retention and swelling of the ankles in some people, especially the elderly. This can cause problems in people who are at risk of congestive heart disease, so heart function may need to be monitored. Tell your doctor if you notice any swelling, breathlessness or weight gain.

- ✔ May cause hypoglycaemia if combined with other medication for diabetes. (They're unlikely to cause hypoglycaemia if used on their own.)

- ✔ May increase the chance of broken bones in the upper arm, hand or foot; while this may be more of a problem if you have osteoporosis, it's always important to do what you can to keep your bones strong.

- ✔ Can worsen macular oedema; make sure you have your regular eye checks and tell your doctor if you notice changes in your vision.

In addition to the possible side effects included in the preceding list, rosiglitazone has been associated with the possibility of an increased risk of death from heart attack in people taking the drug; for this reason, its use is now carefully monitored. Also, Rosiglitazone isn't approved for use with insulin. If pioglitazone is used with insulin, it needs to be monitored closely due to the chance of fluid retention and heart failure.

Studies have shown that no dosage adjustments are required in patients with kidney impairment.

A related thiazolidinedione drug, troglitazone, was taken off the market because it caused liver damage in some people. Rosiglitazone and pioglitazone seem to be free of these liver problems. However, before starting treatment, you should have a liver function test to measure your liver enzymes, and then have these tested periodically.

Glitazone drugs shouldn't be taken by women who are pregnant or breastfeeding.

Unexpected side effects, such as unintended pregnancies, have occurred in women of child-bearing age who take glitazones. As a consequence of insulin resistance, many such women have reduced fertility; when they take glitazones, their fertility may improve and they may become pregnant.

Generally, glitazones are used in conjunction with other oral hypoglycaemic agents. This type of regimen is initiated in people with type 2 diabetes in whom diet and exercise and other tablets aren't successful and the blood glucose is still mildly to moderately elevated.

Repaglinide

Repaglinide, brand name Novonorm, belongs to the group of drugs called *meglitinides*, which are chemically unrelated to the sulphonylureas but work by squeezing more insulin out of the pancreas, just like the sulphonylureas do. Repaglinide, however, is taken just before meals to stimulate insulin for only that meal.

The characteristics of repaglinide are that it

✔ Has a starting dose of 0.5 milligrams with a mild elevation of blood glucose or 1 or 2 milligrams if the initial blood glucose is higher; the dose may be doubled once a week to a maximum of 4 milligrams before meals (daily maximum of 12 milligrams). Take the medication just before or up to 30 minutes before meals; if you're skipping a meal, don't take the tablet.

✔ Can cause hypoglycaemia, because it acts through insulin

✔ Isn't recommended for use in women who are pregnant or breastfeeding

✔ Shouldn't be used with the sulphonylureas but can be combined with metformin; use in combination with rosiglitazone or pioglitazone hasn't been studied

✔ Lowers the blood glucose and the HbA1c effectively when used in combination with metformin

✔ Is mostly broken down in the liver and leaves the body in the bowel movement; if liver disease is present, the dose has to be adjusted downward

✔ Must be monitored closely when used by people with kidney impairment, despite the lack of excretion through the kidneys, with increases in the dose made more carefully

✔ Is expensive, because this drug is only available on a private script

Dipeptidyl peptidase-IV inhibitors

The dipeptidyl peptidase-IV (DPP-IV) inhibitors belong to the newest group of drugs available for type 2 diabetes called *incretin enhancers*. When you eat food, hormones called incretins are secreted from the gut. Incretins stimulate the pancreas to produce insulin and reduce the amount of glucose made by the liver. The DPP-IV inhibitors slow the breakdown of incretins so they can work more effectively. At the time of writing, two members of this group are available in Australia on the Pharmaceutical Benefits Scheme with an authority prescription:

- **Sitaliptin** (brand name Januvia) is usually taken as a 100-milligram dose once daily, with or without food; it's mainly excreted in the urine (doses are reduced if kidney function is impaired). Also comes as a combination tablet with metformin (marketed as Janumet), which is taken twice daily with or after food.

- **Vildagliptin** (brand name Galvus) comes in 50 milligram tablets, can be taken once or twice daily with or without food, and shouldn't be used by people with renal impairment.

Because DPP-IV inhibitors are a new class of medication, the long-term safety is unknown. Some known adverse effects include the following:

- Allergic reactions such as a rash or swelling have been reported (although rarely); see you doctor if you notice any such symptoms

- Headaches

- Infections of the *nasopharyngeal* area (the area of the throat behind the nose) and upper respiratory tract infections, which produce symptoms similar to a cold

- Pancreatitis has been reported but whether it was caused by these medications is unclear

Because the DPP-IV inhibitors only work in response to food, they're unlikely to cause hypoglycaemia when used with metformin; however, the chance of hypoglycaemia is greater if combined with a sulphonylurea. They have a neutral effect on weight.

Combining oral agents

Sometimes the characteristics of the currently available
oral agents don't provide the tight control needed to avoid
complications (particularly true after many years of type 2
diabetes). In this case, insulin may be required, and it may be
added in a number of ways. Often an injection of long-acting
insulin at bedtime is all that's needed to start the day under
control and continue it with oral agents. Tablets may control
the daytime glucose very well after eating, but the first morning
glucose may need the overnight injection of insulin.

As type 2 diabetes progresses, the oral agents may be less
effective, and insulin is taken more often. Two injections
per day of a premixed insulin may do the trick. Usually you
take two-thirds of the dose in the morning and one-third before
dinner — because you need rapid-acting insulin to control the
dinner carbohydrates. This combination is especially valuable in
elderly people with diabetes where the tightest level of control
isn't being sought because the expected lifespan of the person
is shorter than the time necessary to develop complications.
In this person, doctors want to prevent problems like frequent
urination leading to loss of sleep, or vaginal infections, so they
give enough insulin to treat this but not so much that this frail,
elderly patient is having hypoglycaemia on a frequent basis.
Alternatively, a rapid-acting insulin may be added at mealtimes.

When a second injection of insulin is needed, tablets from
the sulphonylureas or repaglinide group of drugs are usually
stopped. Because the pancreas is no longer able to make enough
insulin, these drugs are unable to work well enough. At this
point, metformin is continued to keep working on the person's
insulin sensitivity and so minimise the dose of insulin needed.

Getting Under Your Skin: Injecting Incretin Mimetics

A new group of drugs available for people with type 2 diabetes
is the *incretin mimetics*. When you eat food, incretin hormones
stimulate the pancreas to produce insulin and reduce the
production of glucagon, resulting in an increase in glucose
uptake by muscle and a reduction in the amount of glucose
made by the liver. Artificial incretin mimetics work by copying
this process.

Exenatide (marketed in Australia as Byetta) is one of these agents. The drug results in increased insulin production in response to food, a reduction in glucose made by the liver, and a slowing of glucose absorption by slowing stomach emptying and reducing appetite. It is associated with a small weight loss. Unlike the DPP inhibitors (refer to the section 'Dipeptidyl peptidase-IV inhibitors' earlier in this chapter), exenatide is only available as a *subcutaneous* (beneath the skin) injection. The dose is 5 to 10 milligram injected under the skin one hour *before* breakfast and dinner; it shouldn't be used after a meal. It should be stored in the fridge and each pen contains enough to last for a month.

Because exenatide is a new medication, the long-term safety is unknown at the time of writing. Short-term effects such as nausea, vomiting and diarrhoea are known to be common, but for many people these symptoms settle down in a week or two. Starting with a small dose and increasing after a few weeks also helps reduce these short-term effects. Pancreatitis and kidney problems have been rarely reported but whether they were caused by exenatide is as yet unknown. Hypoglycaemia is unlikely unless exenatide is used in combination with a sulphonylurea. Because it slows stomach emptying, it can affect the absorption of other medicines; take other medicines one hour before taking exenatide to reduce this effect.

Unfortunately, some people need to stop taking exenatide because the nausea caused by the drug doesn't disappear and this side effect is too unpleasant for them to tolerate. If this happens to you, see your doctor to discuss alternatives — don't just stop taking the drug!

Introducing Insulin

If you have type 2 diabetes, you may need insulin late in the course of your disease. Insulin is a great drug, but it must be injected under the skin at the present time.

Reviewing the types of insulin

In the human body, insulin is constantly responding to ups and downs in the blood glucose. No simple device is yet available to measure the blood glucose and deliver insulin as the pancreas does. In order to copy the body's production of insulin as closely as possible, different forms of insulin were developed to work in different time frames. These forms of insulin include

- ✔ **Rapid onset, ultra short-acting insulin (Humalog (lispro) manufactured by Eli Lilly, NovoRapid (aspart) from Novo Nordisk and Apidra (glulisine) from Sanofi Aventis):** The rapid-acting insulins begin to lower the glucose within five minutes after administration, peak at about one hour, and are no longer active after four to five hours. This is a great advance because it frees people with diabetes to allow them to inject just when they eat. With the previous short-acting insulin (neutral insulin), a person had to inject and wait to eat for 30 minutes (hardly convenient!). Because their activity begins and ends so quickly, rapid-acting insulins don't cause hypoglycaemia as often as the earlier preparations.

- ✔ **Short-acting neutral or soluble insulin (Actrapid from Novo Nordisk, Humulin R from Eli Lilly and Hypurin Neutral from Aventis):** Neutral insulin takes 30 minutes to start to lower the glucose, peaks at three hours and is gone within six to eight hours. This insulin is the preparation that was used before meals to keep the glucose low until the next meal. These insulins are rapidly fading in popularity because the ultra short-acting insulins suit most people better.

- ✔ **Intermediate-acting Isophane/NPH insulin (Humulin NPH from Eli Lilly and Protaphane from Novo Nordisk):** This form of insulin begins to lower the glucose within two hours of administration and continues its activity for 16 to 24 hours. The purpose of this kind of insulin is to provide a level of active insulin constantly in the body. However, it does contain a distinctive peak in its action, making it less popular for some people now that we have some peakless long-acting insulins.

- ✔ **Long-acting insulins (glargine (Lantus) from Sanofi-Aventis):** Glargine insulin has an onset of between one and two hours after injection. Its activity lasts for 24 hours without a specific peak activity. This assists in controlling the blood glucose levels over the entire day. Because of its smooth and more predictable activity, glargine is less likely to cause low blood glucose levels at night.

- ✔ **Premixed insulins:** These contain combinations of different short- and long-acting insulins in different percentages. These insulins can be helpful for people who have trouble giving multiple daily injections, have poor eyesight or are stable on a preparation that doesn't change.

Understanding common features of all insulins

A few things are common to all insulins:

- ✔ Insulin may be kept at room temperature for four weeks or in the refrigerator until the expiration date printed on the label. After four weeks at room temperature, it should be discarded.

- ✔ Insulin doesn't take too well to excessive heat, such as direct sunlight, or to excessive cold. Protect your insulin against these conditions or it loses its action.

- ✔ You can safely give an insulin injection through clothing.

- ✔ Various needle sizes are available. Talk to your diabetes nurse educator to discuss which type is best for you.

- ✔ Used syringes and needles should be disposed of in an Australian Safety Standards approved sharps container, which is puncture-proof and sealed shut before disposal. These containers can be obtained from the Australian Diabetes Council (in NSW), Diabetes Australia offices in other states, and some local councils, depending on which state or territory you live in.

Where you inject the insulin helps to determine how predictably it works. For example, insulin injected into the abdomen is absorbed more regularly and in a more predictable way. If you inject into the arms and legs or the buttocks, this predictability is lost and other factors (such as how much the area is being exercised) come into play, making blood glucose levels more erratic. Also, if you use the same site repeatedly, the absorption rate may change as you may develop fatty, hard lumps at the injection site.

The accuracy of your insulin dose is dependent on the accuracy of your injection technique. Make sure you rotate where you choose to inject and learn how to give the injection from an expert — a credentialled diabetes nurse educator!

For many people with diabetes, the timing of insulin injections is also important to help make blood glucose control more predictable. Check with your diabetes care team for advice on which of your insulins need to be taken at the same time and which ones you can be more flexible with (if any!).

Travelling with diabetes

When travelling overseas, all people with diabetes — on insulin or not — need a letter from their doctor listing the medications they're on and the current doses. This information can always be requested by customs officials to crosscheck with the medications packed in your luggage. A letter outlining that you have diabetes and are carrying blood glucose testing equipment, needle tips and hypoglycaemia treatment is also a good idea to prevent possible misunderstandings when you're found to have 'pointy things' or volumes greater than 100 millilitres in your hand luggage!

Because each person has a different insulin requirement and long-distance travel arrangements differ, see your endocrinologist or diabetes educator several weeks before travelling to discuss what you should do about your doses when flying.

Many of the insulin companies provide specialised insulated carry bags to keep your insulin cold while travelling, and you can pick some up from your local diabetes centre. Always take more insulin than you think you'll need. If travelling with a companion, split your insulin between you in case your hand luggage gets lost or stolen. Insulin shouldn't be packed in your check-in luggage because the temperature in the hold is too cold and the insulin may freeze. Frozen (and then defrosted) insulin is unusable.

Delivering insulin with a syringe or a pen

Devices for delivering insulin have undergone many changes from when they were first used by people with diabetes. Syringes are very rarely used and have been replaced by insulin pens. The exception to this may be in some hospitals and aged care facilities.

The needle tips have also been subject to vast improvements over the years. The needles now available are extremely fine and come in several lengths. Your diabetes educator can provide you with the most appropriate needles for your individual needs. Needles are supplied free of charge in most Australian states and territories for people with a National Diabetes Services Scheme (NDSS) card (see the section 'Getting Help with the Costs of Diabetes' later in this chapter for more).

Two types of pens are available in Australia:

- ✔ **Pens that you load with a cartridge of insulin.** Types available include NovoPen 3 and 4 for Novo Nordisk insulin cartridges; Humapen, Luxura and Memoir for Lilly insulin cartridges; and ClickSTAR for Sanofi Aventis insulin cartridges.

- ✔ **Disposable pens that are preloaded for you and discarded when the insulin is finished.** Options available in Australia include FlexPen, Innolet or NovoLet for Novo Nordisk insulins; KwikPen for Lilly insulins; and SoloSTAR for Sanofi Aventis insulins.

Not all pen devices come in all types of insulin; you need to work with your GP and diabetes educator to determine which is best for you.

The number of units you have dialled up for use is displayed in a window on the pen. Each unit (or sometimes each set of two units) is accompanied by a clicking sound so that, if you are visually impaired, you can hear the number of units that you've dialled up for delivery. If you dial up too many units, the pen allows you to reset the dial and start again without wasting insulin. All pens contain 300 units of insulin. Depending on the pen, you can deliver up to 80 units of insulin in one go and you screw on a new needle as needed.

Other Common Medications

Minimising the chance of long-term complications of diabetes involves more than just looking after your blood glucose! Good control of blood pressure and blood lipids (cholesterol and other fats) is important and your doctor may suggest medication to help achieve this. Medication may also be prescribed to help reduce the chance of a heart attack or stroke, or to help with weight loss.

Antihypertensives (medicines for lowering blood pressure)

People with diabetes are more likely to have high blood pressure than people without diabetes. Often, diet and lifestyle efforts aren't enough to get blood pressure to the treatment targets (refer to Chapter 5 for more on treatment targets for blood pressure), so medications may be prescribed. Because these medications act slightly differently, they can be combined to work together, meaning you may end up taking three or more medicines from different groups to help you achieve a target blood pressure.

Some common blood pressure medicines are

- ✔ **ACE inhibitors.** These medicines reduce the amount of a chemical called angiotensin in the body, allowing the blood vessels to relax and widen to reduce blood pressure. They may raise potassium levels, and/or cause a dry cough and an allergic reaction; talk with your doctor if you notice swelling, a rash or any other symptom that you think may be related to your medication. ACE inhibitors are particularly useful in diabetes because they can reduce the progression of kidney disease.

- ✔ **Angiotensin receptor blockers.** Like ACE inhibitors, this group also reduces the amount of angiotensin in the body, but at a different point. Angiotensin receptor blockers have similar side effects to ACE inhibitors, although the allergies are less likely to occur. They also reduce the progression of kidney disease in diabetes.

- ✔ **Beta blockers.** These medicines work by blocking beta one receptors in the heart, reducing the work done by the heart and stopping the blood vessels from tightening. Beta blockers can cause breathlessness in people with asthma and mask some signs of hypoglycaemia.

- ✔ **Calcium channel blockers.** These medicines block the use of calcium in the blood vessels, allowing them to relax. They have been shown to cause ankle swelling; if you notice this symptom, ask your doctor about taking a different blood pressure medication.

- ✔ **Thiazide and related diuretics (fluid tablets).** When used in low doses for blood pressure, these medications work mainly by relaxing blood vessels. They can cause too many salts, such as potassium, to be lost in the urine; talk to your doctor about monitoring these levels if you're on this medication.

All antihypertensive medications can cause low blood pressure, so be careful particularly when getting up from lying down or sitting.

Drugs for dyslipidemia (abnormal levels of fats in the blood)

In addition to switching to a low-fat diet and increasing exercise, medication may also be required to manage the levels of fats in your blood; several different groups of medicines are now available to do this. Again, you may need to be on more than one type of medication to help you reach your desired targets.

Drugs commonly available to help with lowering the levels of fats in your blood include the following:

- **Ezetimibe.** This medication works by blocking the absorption of cholesterol in the gut. Like the statins (refer to the last item in this list), ezetimibe may also cause muscle pain, weakness and diarrhoea.

- **Fibrates.** This group of medication works mainly by reducing triglyceride levels (one of the damaging fats; refer to Chapter 5 for more on the different types of fats). Fibrates can also cause muscle pain or weakness, liver reactions, sensitivity to sun exposure and stomach upsets.

- **Fish Oils.** Fish oils contain two active ingredients: Eicosapentaenoic acid (EPA) and docosahexaenoic acid (DHA), which can lower triglyceride levels in the blood. To be effective, you need to take 1.2 to 5 grams of these active ingredients each day.

- **Statins.** This group is also known as *HMG-CoA reductase inhibitors* because they block the HMG-CoA reductase enzyme, needed for making cholesterol in the body. These medications can cause a rise in liver enzymes, muscle pain or weakness.

Antiplatelet medication

These medicines are used to reduce the likelihood of clots forming in your blood vessels, which could result in a heart attack or a stroke. Antiplatelet medications include the following:

- **Aspirin.** Used in doses of 100 milligram or 150 milligram once per day, this medication can be bought over the counter without a prescription. Aspirin may cause stomach upsets and increase the likelihood of bleeding.

✔ **Clopidogrel.** This medication may be used if you can't tolerate aspirin or if you have another heart condition. A 75-milligram tablet is taken once daily.

Weight-loss medication

People with type 2 diabetes are often overweight or obese, and so, in conjunction with a low-kilojoule diet high in fruit and vegetables and increased exercise, may also be prescribed medications to help with weight loss.

The only scientifically proven weight-loss medications available in Australia at the time of writing that we would recommend are orlistat (marketed as Xenical), which works by blocking the absorption of dietary fat in the gut and phentermine (marketed as Duromine or Metermine), which is a sympathetic nervous system stimulant with some appetite suppressant activity.

Weight-loss drugs only work while you take them. As soon as you stop taking them, your body returns to normal and, unless you can continue a low-kilojoule diet without the help of the drugs, you often put any weight lost straight back on.

See Chapter 8 for more discussion on diet and the use and effectiveness of weight-loss medications.

Avoiding Drug Interactions

A person with diabetes may be taking several different drugs, which may interact and cause drug toxicity problems. If your doctor prescribes a medication, make sure to ask your doctor to check whether it can interact with other medications you're taking or can raise blood glucose levels.

Get to know the names of all the drugs you take (both the brand names and the names of the medicine it contains) and whether they affect one another. Refer to *Diabetes For Dummies*, *3rd Australian Edition*, for a full list of drugs that may raise blood glucose levels.

Some common drugs or medications also lower the blood glucose. The most important of these include alcohol, high doses of aspirin, Gemfibrozil and the antibiotic trimethoprim.

Getting Help with the Costs of Diabetes

Diabetes can be expensive, especially if you need several drugs to control your blood glucose. Many diabetes medications have been listed on the government-funded Pharmaceutical Benefits Scheme, which provides drugs at subsidised prices. Most diabetes medications (including insulin and some oral hypoglycaemic agents) are listed on the scheme. Others, such as repaglinide, aren't, which makes them very expensive options.

Some medications may be available in cheaper brands, often called *generics*. They contain the same medication and have to meet the same Australian standards, so are safe to take for most people.

Diabetes Australia operates the Commonwealth Government's National Diabetes Services Scheme (NDSS), which subsidises the cost of test strips and provides free needles and syringes. You can register at the Australian Diabetes Council (in NSW) or Diabetes Australia in other states. A special form must be signed by your doctor or credentialed diabetes educator to receive a free benefits card. All people with diabetes who have a Medicare card are entitled to be registered with the NDSS scheme and receive the associated discounts.

Members of the Australian Diabetes Council (in NSW) and Diabetes Australia (in other states) also receive discounts on items that people with diabetes need, such as glucose tablets, foot moisturisers, swabs, glucose meters and control solutions, insulin-injecting devices, recipe and informative books, and videos.

Your health insurance company may also provide rebates on meters, depending on your level of cover.

Chapter 8

Healthy Eating in Diabetes

. . . .

In This Chapter

▶ Working out an appropriate kilojoule intake

▶ Understanding carbohydrates

▶ Picking proteins and avoiding fats

▶ Checking your intake of vitamins, minerals and water

▶ Knowing how your diabetes is affected by alcohol

▶ Planning balanced meals

▶ Taking action to check and reduce your weight

. . . .

*I*n this chapter, you find out much that you need to know to make your diet work for you — not only to improve your diabetes and control your blood glucose, but also to feel that you have an improved quality of life. Every person is unique, however, so make sure you also see a specialist diabetes dietitian, who can give you individualised advice.

Because most people with type 2 diabetes are overweight, weight management and reduction should be the major consideration. The good news is, if you are overweight, you benefit from even a small weight loss. Weight loss markedly reduces the risk of developing type 2 diabetes and prevents the progression of prediabetes (refer to Chapter 3) to type 2 diabetes. It can also reverse the failure to respond to drugs for diabetes that develops after responding at first (refer to Chapter 7 for more on medications). Weight loss can increase life expectancy, help lower blood pressure and improve energy levels and mobility.

The benefits of weight loss are seen rapidly, even when relatively little weight has been lost. A rapid fall in blood glucose occurs as soon as the energy intake of the diet is reduced. Over time, the blood pressure declines and the cholesterol falls.

The triglycerides drop and the good cholesterol (HDL) rises. Even a modest reduction of 10 per cent of body weight has a significant positive effect on your coronary artery disease risk.

Unfortunately, your genetic make-up has a significant influence on your ability to lose weight and on the amount of weight you lose. Several studies have shown that people with type 2 diabetes lose less weight than people without diabetes. This can be disheartening and frustrating — especially when trying to explain not being able to lose weight to less-than-sympathetic workmates, family, friends or (we hate to say) health professionals. But, hang in there — even when weight loss isn't possible, weight maintenance is an excellent goal, and you can certainly implement measures to improve the quality of your diet, weight loss or not.

Examining Your Kilojoule Intake

Helen Jacobs, a 46-year-old office worker, was a new patient with type 2 diabetes who came to her endocrinologist because of high blood glucose levels, blurring of her vision and numbness in her toes. She was 1.65 metres tall and weighed 84.8 kilograms. This gave her a body mass index of 30.9 — putting her just in the obese range. (See the section 'Checking your weight' later in this chapter for more.) She was taking tablets for her diabetes. Her GP had told her she needed to lose weight and referred her to her local specialist diabetes dietitian. Helen started on a healthy eating plan, reducing the amount of saturated fat, increasing fibre and reducing the portion size of her meals. Her plan also included increasing her levels of physical activity to offset her sedentary job. She followed her plan and lost 8 kilograms, which she has kept off. Her blood glucose is now in the range of 6.1 to 8.0 mmol/L most of the time. She no longer has blurring of vision, and her toes are beginning to improve. Her endocrinologist has reduced Helen's diabetes medication and she feels much better. Her GP is now looking after her diabetes because the specialist doesn't need to see her for a year.

No matter how you cut it, your weight is determined by the number of kilojoules you take in, minus the number of kilojoules you use up by exercise. If more kilojoules come in, you gain weight. If fewer kilojoules come in than go out, you lose weight. Kilojoule needs are different for different ages, different sexes and different levels of activity — for example, if a woman is pregnant or breastfeeding, she needs more kilojoules. However, a basic principle remains: If a person is trying to lose weight, reducing the total kilojoules per day can help achieve this. Like Helen, you may do even better if you can increase your level of physical activity — see Chapter 9 for more help in this area.

Try to identify around 2,000 kilojoules that you can remove from your diet per day. By removing this number of kilojoules, you can lose around 0.5 kilograms per week. The fewer kilojoules you remove, the slower your weight loss will be.

Three basic food groups contain kilojoules: Carbohydrates, proteins and fats. The following sections cover these main groups, highlighting which are the best choices in each group to help you meet your long-term health goals.

Considering Carbohydrates

Specialists recommend that carbohydrate that's high in fibre and low in fat should contribute between 40 and 50 per cent of your total daily kilojoule intake. An important part of achieving this target is avoiding the sources of carbohydrates that contain lots of kilojoules, but offer little nutritional value.

You probably already have some idea about which carbohydrates only provide 'empty' kilojoules. Some examples include cakes, biscuits, sweet pastries, honey, jam, ice-cream and sweet yoghurt, lollies, chocolate, soft drinks, cordials and sugar added to drinks and breakfast cereal. (Alcohol also contains kilojoules — see the section 'Considering the Effect of Alcohol' later in this chapter for more.)

The best carbohydrate choices for you are those that are highest in fibre and lowest in fat — studies have shown that a diet featuring these types of foods can lower blood glucose and cholesterol levels.

Fibre is the part of a food that's not digestible and so adds no kilojoules but has health benefits. Fibre is found in all fruits, vegetables and cereal grains, and the more unprocessed the grain (or fruit or vegetable), the higher the fibre content.

Checking the glycaemic index

By avoiding carbohydrates that are high in kilojoules but low in nutritional value, you significantly reduce your intake of sugar (glucose), lowering your blood glucose levels very rapidly. As well as this, choosing foods high in fibre is a good way to satisfy hunger (although not the only way — see the section 'Choosing Proteins' later in this chapter for more on this). Foods high in fibre also tend to have a lower glycaemic index.

 The glycaemic index (GI) is a measure of how fast a carbohydrate food is digested. Slowly digested carbohydrate foods release their glucose into the bloodstream more slowly, leaving the pancreas more time to provide the right amount of insulin.

The lower the GI of a food, the better, but the quantity eaten is still important. Foods that are excellent sources of carbohydrate but have a low GI include legumes such as lentils, split peas or beans, pasta, grains like barley, basmati rice and some wholegrain breads.

 Because carbohydrates such as breads, pasta and breakfasts cereals often make up a large portion of your daily intake, switching to low-GI options in these areas can make a major difference in the overall GI of your diet and so on your blood glucose levels. Here are some ways you can easily substitute a high GI food with a low GI food; try substituting:

- ✔ Heavily grained bread (examples include Bürgen varieties and Tip Top 9 Grain) for white or wholemeal bread.

- ✔ Unrefined cereals such as oats or processed low-GI cereals (examples include Guardian and All-Bran cereals) for processed breakfast cereal.

- ✔ Pasta, Carisma potatoes, sweet corn or legumes for regular potatoes.

- ✔ Basmati, doongara or other low-GI rice for jasmine or arborio rice.

- ✔ Temperate-climate fruits such as apples and plums for tropical fruits such as bananas.

- ✔ Biscuits made with dried fruits or whole grains such as oats for plain biscuits or crackers.

You can't always tell whether a food is low GI just by looking at it — for example, the puffing or flattening of grains that occurs during the production of many breakfast cereals can raise the GI of the food, whereas mixing flour and water, rolling, drying and then cooking it (that's pasta!) lowers the GI. To check a food's GI, consult the GI tables available on various websites — but just make sure the site you're looking at is Australian.

 Even though a food is low GI, you still may have to avoid it if you're trying to reduce your kilojoule intake — or not eat as much of it as you'd like. Low-GI food can be high in fat, so make sure you also check food's fat content before assuming it's appropriate. Portion size is also important — even if the food is low GI and low in fat, you can't eat large portions and still lose weight!

Spreading out your carbohydrate choices

Even carbohydrates with low-GI ratings (see preceding section) can eventually raise your blood glucose levels because carbo-hydrates (that is, starches and sugars) are made from glucose.

Because of this, people often think that they should avoid all carbohydrate foods; however, you need some glucose to provide your brain and muscles with the fuel they need to function well. The key to living more healthily is in knowing how much carbohydrate to consume, and when.

You need to limit the total amount of carbohydrate in your diet and also spread it fairly evenly across the day to maintain healthy blood glucose levels. For most people with type 2 diabetes, the best approach is to have three main meals per day, each containing a moderate amount of carbohydrate, and to have these meals at regular times.

 Some people may require snacks in addition to their three main meals each day due to the type of medication they're on. Your diabetes dietitian can advise you on the most appropriate spread of carbohydrate across the day for you.

Choosing Proteins

Protein is used by the body for growing and repairing tissues. For this reason, it was thought that you could build your own muscle by eating lots of protein (actually, you build up muscle by exercising). Although children and young adults need more protein because they're growing, adults need relatively little in order to maintain their current level of muscle.

Protein in your diet comes from chicken, pork, beef, kangaroo, lamb, eggs, milk and other dairy foods, nuts and legumes (or pulses). The protein component of these foods doesn't raise blood glucose levels.

Your choice of protein is still very important because some protein sources are very high in fat (usually saturated fat) whereas some are relatively fat-free. Wherever possible, you should choose lean types of protein foods because in these foods you get more protein than fat, making the energy (or kilojoule) content for these foods lower. For example, having 100 grams of salami on your sandwich provides you with 1,733 kilojoules just in the salami. By substituting that with 100 grams of lean roast beef, you get 736 kilojoules (and much less salt!).

For most adults, two moderate-sized serves of protein per day are sufficient. Because milk, yoghurt and legumes are sources of protein and carbohydrate, they can be included in the diet to satisfy your requirements for both food types.

A certain amount of controversy surrounds the question of how much protein should be in the diet. Most international recommendations state that protein should contribute between 10 and 20 per cent of your total daily kilojoules. However, some studies show that protein is more likely to satisfy your hunger, so a little higher percentage of protein in your diet can help your weight-loss efforts.

We don't recommend that anyone removes all carbohydrate from their diet and replaces it with protein foods. You need a balanced diet, not one that is overloaded with one food type or nutrient. For adults, about a quarter of your plate should be covered by the protein part of your meal.

The following lists give you an idea of the fat content of various sources of protein. If you choose your protein from the very lean and lean categories as often as possible, and cut down on some of your carbohydrate intake, you can still achieve your weight-loss goals. (In the next section, we explain the different kinds of fats.)

Examples of *very lean* meat, fish or substitutes include

- ✔ Lean veal, beef, pork or lamb (grilled or baked)
- ✔ Legumes (such as soya beans and lentils)
- ✔ Lobster, prawns and crab
- ✔ Skim/low-fat milk, low-fat yoghurt and cottage cheese
- ✔ Skinless white chicken meat or turkey (grilled or baked)
- ✔ Tofu or Quorn (a vegetarian protein source made from fungi similar to mushrooms)
- ✔ White fish or tuna canned in brine or spring water

Lean meat, fish or substitute options include the following:

- ✔ An egg
- ✔ Bacon (fat-trimmed and grilled)
- ✔ Dark chicken meat without skin (grilled or baked)
- ✔ Ricotta cheese
- ✔ Salmon canned in brine or tuna canned in oil
- ✔ Soya beans

Examples of *high-fat* meat or substitutes include

- ✔ Cheddar, blue vein, camembert, feta and cream cheeses
- ✔ Nuts
- ✔ Processed meats, such as sausages, salami, devon and mortadella

See the section 'Putting It All Together: Planning Meals' later in this chapter for more on incorporating the right sorts of protein choices into your diet.

If you're unsure about the mix of carbohydrates and proteins that's right for you, see your specialist diabetes dietitian for an individualised assessment.

Monitoring the Fat in Your Diet

Very little disagreement exists among scientists and researchers about the need to limit fat intake! Everyone agrees that you should eat no more than 30 per cent of your diet as fats. As with protein (refer to the preceding section), the type of fat that you eat needs to be considered as well as the quantity.

Dietary fat comes in several forms:

- ✔ **Saturated** fat is the kind of fat that mainly comes from animal sources. For example, the streaks of fat in a steak are saturated fat; butter is made up of saturated fat. Bacon, cream, cheese, pastries, cakes, biscuits and chocolate are other examples that contain saturated fat. Two non-animal sources of saturated fat exist: Palm oil and coconut milk. Eating a lot of saturated fat increases the blood cholesterol level.

- ✔ **Unsaturated** fat comes from vegetable sources such as nuts and seeds. It comes in several forms:

  - • **Monounsaturated** fat doesn't raise cholesterol. Avocado, olive oil, canola oil, olive and canola spreads are examples. The oil in nuts like almonds and peanuts is monounsaturated.

  - • **Polyunsaturated** fat also doesn't raise cholesterol but does cause a reduction in the good or HDL cholesterol. Examples of polyunsaturated fats are soft fats and oils such as sunflower, soybean, sesame oil, oily fish (trout) and sunflower spread.

Although 30 per cent of your total daily kilojoules should come from fat, less than one-third of this amount should come from saturated fats.

Protection against heart disease comes from including essential fatty acids, found in fish oils, in your diet. If you dislike fish — or just can't eat the required two to three serves of it each week — fish oil capsules are a good substitute. Just make sure when buying the capsules that they contain sufficient quantities of the two active ingredients *eicosapentaenoic acid* (EPA) and *docosahexaenoic acid* (DHA). It is recommended you take between 1,200 milligrams and 3,000 milligrams of a combination of these active ingredients each day. To make it easier, many formulations of fish oil are now concentrated, meaning you only need to take one or two capsules per day to reach the 1,200 milligrams per day target.

Getting Enough Vitamins, Minerals and Water

Your diet must contain sufficient vitamins and minerals for good health, but the amount you need may be less than you think. If you eat a balanced diet that comes from the various food groups, you generally get enough vitamins for your daily needs. Table 8-1 lists the vitamins and their food sources.

Table 8-1	Vitamins You Need	
Vitamin	*Function*	*Food Source*
Vitamin A	Needed for growth and development, immune function, bones and healthy skin; helps with night vision	Liver, eggs, oily fish, dairy products, orange and green vegetables and orange fruits
Vitamin B1 (thiamine)	Converts carbohydrate into energy	Wholegrain cereals, meat, fish, nuts and yeast extract
Vitamin B2 (riboflavin)	Needed to release energy from food	Milk, cheese, fish, almonds, eggs, green vegetables and fortified cereals
Vitamin B6 (pyridoxine), pantothenic acid and biotin	Needed for growth, normal brain and nerve function	Bananas, potatoes, wholegrain cereals, meat, fish and nuts
Vitamin B12	Keeps the red blood cells and the nervous system healthy	Animal foods only; for example, meat, seafood, eggs
Folic acid	Keeps the red blood cells and the nervous system healthy	Liver, fortified breakfast cereals, green leafy vegetables and yeast extract
Niacin	Helps release energy	Meat, chicken, fish, nuts, legumes and wholegrain products
Vitamin C	Helps maintain supportive tissues	Fruit and some vegetables; for example, tomatoes and capsicum

(continued)

Table 8-1 (continued)

Vitamin	Function	Food Source
Vitamin D	Helps with absorption of calcium	Oily fish, egg yolk and fortified milk and margarines; also made in the skin when exposed to sunlight, although this process declines as you age
Vitamin E	Helps maintain cells	Vegetable oils, nuts, seeds and wholegrain cereals
Vitamin K	Needed for proper clotting of the blood	Green leafy vegetables; also made by bacteria in your intestine

As you look through the vitamins in Table 8-1, you can see that most of them are easily available in the foods you eat every day. (In certain situations, such as during pregnancy, you may need to take a vitamin or mineral supplement to ensure that you're getting enough every day.)

As far as vitamins are concerned, proof just doesn't exist that large amounts are beneficial. In some cases, they may be harmful. We don't recommend that you take megadoses of vitamins. Vitamin D deficiency is more common in obesity or in people who are veiled or indoors a lot, and may need checking.

Minerals are also key ingredients of a healthy diet. Most are needed in tiny amounts, which, with a few exceptions, are easily consumed from a balanced diet. These essential minerals are as follows:

✔ **Calcium, phosphorous and magnesium build bones and teeth.** Milk and other dairy products provide plenty of these minerals, but evidence suggests that people aren't getting enough calcium. The recommended intake for adults is 1,000 milligrams. Women over 50 years and men over 70 years are recommended to have 1,300 milligrams each day. Pregnant women and breastfeeding mothers should have 1,000 milligrams, particularly in the final three months of the pregnancy and throughout the breastfeeding period.

✔ **Iodine is essential for production of thyroid hormones.** Iodine is often added to salt in order to ensure that people get enough of it. In many areas of the world where iodine is not found in the soil, people suffer from very large thyroid glands known as goitres.

✔ **Iron is essential for red blood cells.** Iron is obtained from red meat and iron-fortified breakfast cereals. Green leafy vegetables provide small amounts of iron; however, it's not in a form that's easily absorbed by the body. A menstruating woman loses iron each month and may need to supplement her food with a tablet. Vegetarians and pregnant or breastfeeding mothers may also require a supplement.

✔ **Sodium regulates body water.** You really need only about 300 milligrams of sodium per day but may take in 20 to 40 times that much, which probably explains a lot of the high blood pressure in Australia. Don't add salt to your food because it already has plenty in it — and you'll enjoy the taste a lot more without it.

✔ **Chromium is needed in tiny amounts.** No scientific evidence shows that chromium is especially helpful to the person with diabetes in controlling the blood glucose, despite reams of articles in health food magazines to the contrary.

✔ Various other minerals, like **chlorine, cobalt, tin** and **zinc** are found in many foods. These minerals are essential but are rarely lacking in the human diet.

Water is the last important nutrient mentioned in this section, but it's by no means the least important. Your body is made up of 60 per cent water and all the nutrients in your body are dissolved in it. You need to drink about six to eight glasses, or one and a half to two litres, of fluid per day — more if the weather is very hot or you're exercising a lot. Your thirst will tell you how much you need.

Considering the Effect of Alcohol

Alcohol is high in kilojoules but offers no particular nutritional value, although it has been shown that a moderate amount (a small glass or two of wine a day) may reduce the risk of heart attack. Unfortunately, alcohol is often taken to excess and does major damage to the body; it can damage the liver, brain and pancreas (where insulin comes from!).

Because alcohol has kilojoules, if you drink some, you must consider it as extra kilojoules in your diet. Replacing food kilojoules with alcohol kilojoules may mean your diet becomes inadequate in valuable vitamins and minerals. If you drink alcohol, limit your intake to no more than two standard drinks five out of seven days per week. In Australia, a standard drink is the volume of an alcoholic beverage that provides 10 grams of alcohol.

The kilojoule content of one standard drink from the more common alcoholic beverages is

- 30 millilitres of most spirits contain 252 kilojoules
- 60 millilitres of dry sherry contain 252 kilojoules
- 100 millilitres of red or white wine contain 285 kilojoules
- 60 millilitres of port or sweet sherry contain 378 kilojoules
- 285 millilitres of full-strength beer contain 491 kilojoules
- 425 millilitres of low-alcohol beer contain 438 kilojoules

In addition to the kilojoules, alcohol plays other roles in diabetes. If alcohol is taken without food, it can cause low blood glucose by increasing the effect of insulin without food to compensate. In those with type 2 diabetes, hypoglycaemia after drinking alcohol is less common and usually would only occur in someone taking sulphonylureas or insulin to control blood glucose levels (refer to Chapter 7 for more on medications).

Putting It All Together: Planning Meals

A balanced diet contains regular amounts of carbohydrates, proteins and fats with sufficient variety to provide you with all the vitamins and minerals you require for health. To give you an idea of the types and quantities of foods you should aim to be eating, the following lists your daily targets, broken into carbohydrates, proteins, fats and your vitamin- and mineral-rich essentials.

Meals should be spread across the day but only some adults require snacks in addition to their three main meals. When selecting carbohydrates, keep in mind the following:

- ✔ This group includes bread, potato, rice and other grains, pasta, fruit, breakfast cereals, milk and yoghurt.

- ✔ Food from this group should provide between 40 and 50 per cent of your energy needs for the day. This equates to two to three serves of carbohydrate at each meal for a small person or someone trying to lose weight or up to twice this much for a lean, large and/or active person.

- ✔ Two to three serves of carbohydrate equates to covering about a quarter of your plate with these foods.

- ✔ One serve of carbohydrates is approximately equal to a slice of bread, a piece of fruit, third of a cup of cooked rice, half a cup of grains, cereals, starchy vegetables or cooked pasta, 200 grams of plain yoghurt, or 300 millilitres of milk.

- ✔ You should aim to choose low-fat, high-fibre options.

- ✔ You should try to have two pieces of fruit each day.

The following factors are important when considering protein food choices:

- ✔ This group includes meat, chicken, fish, eggs, dairy foods, nuts and legumes.

- ✔ Food from this group should make up between 10 and 20 per cent of an adult's diet. This equates to two moderate-sized serves per day for an adult.

- ✔ One small serve of protein is approximately equal to 90 grams of meat or chicken, 150 grams of fish, two large eggs, 40 grams of cheese, 30 grams of nuts or half a cup of cooked legumes.

- ✔ You should aim to choose low-fat varieties.

- ✔ You should cook and prepare these foods with as little added fat (and salt) as possible.

Keep in mind the following when looking at fats in your food choices:

- This group includes butter, margarine, oils, mayonnaise, salad dressings, cream and sour cream.

- Fat should only make up approximately 30 per cent of your diet.

- Your first choice from the fat options should be polyunsaturated or monounsaturated fats, such as margarine and oils.

- Most people don't need more than one tablespoon of added unsaturated fats (such as vegetable margarines and oils) each day, because their carbohydrate and protein choices already contain some fats.

- When buying cooking oils, always choose oils where the source of the oil (such as olive, canola, sunflower or peanut) is labelled.

- You shouldn't be tempted to cut out fat altogether! The human body needs essential fatty acids and fat-soluble vitamins to function well, and these are provided by these fats.

As a bit of a bonus, you also get to choose from what we call free foods. The name says it all, really — these are foods that contain few carbohydrates, fats or proteins, but provide fibre and essential vitamins and minerals to your daily diet. You can go ahead and eat these foods freely to add bulk and interest to your diet!

Keep in mind the following when selecting free foods:

- Options in this group include all vegetables (except potato, sweet potato and sweet corn), lemons, grapefruit, passionfruit and rhubarb.

- At mealtimes, you want half your plate covered by free foods such as vegetables or salad.

- Low-kilojoule foods are also included in this group, such as mustard, pickles, chutney, herbs and spices, Vegemite and oil-free dressings.

Food for thought

The websites listed here cover a wide area of nutrition information, and can provide help on the technical aspects of nutrition as well as the practical requirements of eating, like recipes!

✔ Calorie King: Vast quantities of information on the nutritional value of Australian foods. The site is free to use and also has recipes. www.calorieking.com.au

✔ Dietitians Association of Australia: This site provides information relating to their mission statement: 'Better Food, Better Health, Better Living'. Reviews of seminar presentations are available, as well as scientific papers and abstracts relating to the role of diet in diabetes. www.daa.asn.au

✔ Foods Standards Australia and New Zealand: The Australian Government website containing the official nutritional values of Australian foods. www.foodstandards.gov.au

✔ Glycaemic Index: This is the official Australian glycaemic index site and is linked with the Glycaemic Index Symbol program from the University of Sydney. www.glycemicindex.com

✔ Nutrition Australia: A good site for information about the dietary requirements of diabetes. www.nutritionaustralia.org

✔ Symply Too Good: This site provides great recipes that are easy and delicious. www.symplytoogood.com.au

Losing Weight

If you're overweight or obese, the health benefits of losing even a small amount of weight are large. The following sections help you check your weight, so you know where you are right now, and offer guidance to the various weight-loss methods available.

Checking your weight

To give you a general idea of how much you ought to weigh, you can use a formula called the *body mass index* (BMI), which relates your weight to your height — so if you're shorter than someone who weighs the same as you, you have the higher BMI. A person with a BMI under 20 is considered underweight. A person with a BMI from 20 to 25 is a normal weight. A person with a BMI from 25.1 to 29.9 is overweight, and a person with a

BMI of 30 or over is obese. By this definition, around 66 per cent of people in Australia are overweight or obese.

You can't step on a scale and get a reading of your BMI, but you can get your weight. This is one of the easiest measurements in medicine.

To work out your BMI, take your weight (in kilograms) and divide it by your height (in metres) squared. For example, say you weigh 82 kilograms and are 1.69 metres tall. Your BMI is 82 divided by 2.8561 (1.69 squared), or 28.7 — putting you in the overweight range.

Maintaining a BMI as close as possible to the normal range makes controlling your diabetes and blood pressure easier.

Reducing your weight

Weight reduction is difficult for many reasons. In our experience, most people do very well initially but tend to return to old habits because it's so hard to keep on track all the time. Evidence suggests that this tendency to regain weight is built into the human brain. When fat tissue is decreased or even increased, a central control system in the brain acts to restore the fat to the previous level. If liposuction is done, for example, the remaining cells swell up to hold more fat.

Still, losing weight and keeping it off is possible. It's just very difficult and requires lifelong effort. In Chapter 9, we discuss the value of exercise in a weight-loss program. At this point, you need to realise that successful maintenance of weight loss requires a willingness to make exercise a part of your daily life. If, for some reason, you can't move your legs to exercise, you can get a satisfactory workout using your upper body alone. A recent study showed that 92 per cent of the people who maintained weight loss were exercising regularly, while only 34 per cent of those who regained their weight continued to exercise.

Checking out types of diets

The endless number of diets that are around certainly suggest that no one method is any better than all the others. Some are fairly drastic in the degree to which they cut kilojoules, and weight loss is fairly rapid. However, when you come off one of these quick weight-loss diets, more often than not you quickly put back on all the weight you lost.

 Check with your GP or diabetes care team if you're planning to try a quick weight-loss diet because your diabetes medications may need to be changed.

Among the more drastic diets are the following:

- **Very low kilojoule diets:** On a daily basis, these diets provide 1,600 to 3,300 kilojoules with supplemental vitamins and minerals. They're safe for people with diabetes when supervised by a diabetes dietitian or doctor. They can be used when you need rapid weight loss, such as before an operation. They result in rapid initial weight loss with a fall in the need for medication. Weight restoration commonly occurs, but depends on what dietary pattern and exercise level you follow afterwards. These diets are not easy to follow because you're often required to replace proper meals with a drink or bar. This makes them rather socially unacceptable — and not that attractive when family and friends around you are all eating 'proper' food! However, they can be very useful for some people — just check with your diabetes dietitian or GP first if you think this kind of diet may be a suitable approach for you.

- **Very high protein diets:** Food is limited to animal protein sources in an effort to maintain body protein, meaning the diet contains very little carbohydrate. A supplement with a full complement of vitamins and minerals should be taken when following these diets. Patients often complain of tiredness, constipation and bad breath. Weight is regained rapidly when the diet is discontinued. This diet is not balanced and we don't recommend it for more than a few weeks.

- **Fasts:** A *fast* means giving up all food for a period of time and taking only water and vitamins and minerals. A fast is such a drastic change from normal eating habits that people don't remain on the fast for very long, and the weight lost is usually quickly regained. These diets can be dangerous and should be avoided.

Several diets are associated with large organisations that often require you to purchase only their foods. The support given by some of these organisations seems to be extremely helpful in weight loss maintenance. In addition, the slower loss of weight and the similarity of the diet to normal eating habits seem to result in a greater tendency to stay with the program and keep the weight off. However, people who go on a weight-loss program need to understand that they will regain the weight if they don't make permanent changes to their lifestyle.

As organisations and groups offering weight-loss programs proliferated, some of them far from reputable, the need to regulate the weight loss industry arose. The Weight Management Code Administration Council of Australia administers a code of practice for the industry. The code of practice ensures truthful advertising with authentic success stories, accurate information (including complete cost proposals) and an overall reliable and safe service. An organisation can become a member of the council and is then bound by the code.

The leading contenders in Australia for this type of diet are Jenny Craig, Lite n' Easy and Weight Watchers but the costs of these programs covered are prohibitive for some people, so working with a specialist diabetes dietitian may be a better option for you. Dietitian services can be accessed free of charge through your state or territory health department, or visits to a private dietitian can be subsidised by Medicare. (Government-funded access to dietitians requires a referral from a GP.)

Taking medications

Because most people with type 2 diabetes are struggling with their weight and their glucose control improves with weight loss, the search for weight-lowering drugs has been enthusiastic, to say the least.

The most commonly used weight-loss medication in the Australia is orlistat, which is marketed as Xenical. Orlistat is a *gastrointestinal lipase inhibitor*, which means that it reduces the absorption of fat in the diet. If you eat too much fat, it remains in the intestine, reaches the stool, and can cause flatulence, oily bowel movements and even bowel incontinence. Because of these side effects, some people stop taking the drug. However, such side effects disappear when the fat content of the diet is sufficiently low. This is how it works — it forces you to maintain your low-fat (and therefore low-kilojoule) diet! Otherwise, the consequences can be unpleasant, to say the least.

In a study specifically for people with diabetes, a group using orlistat lost much more weight than a non-orlistat group. The orlistat users were able to reduce their blood glucose, their haemoglobin A1c and their need for oral sulphonylurea medication, as well as their elevated cholesterol levels. Very few of the orlistat-takers stopped taking the drug and left the study because of intestinal or bowel problems. Orlistat could be a major new weapon against the obesity that worsens the effects of diabetes and threatens coronary artery disease. However, its use may be limited by the fact that it is expensive. You can buy orlistat over the counter at pharmacies. (Refer to Chapter 7 for more on medications for weight loss.)

Undergoing surgery

Surgery for weight reduction is used in the more severe cases of obesity. Surgery can have impressive effects such as correction of high glucose levels and reduction or discontinuation of glucose-lowering drugs. Some of the reasons for considering surgical procedures to treat obesity are as follows:

- ✔ You have a BMI that's greater than 35.

- ✔ You have an obesity-related physical problem limiting your ability to walk.

- ✔ You have an obesity-related health problem like diabetes.

- ✔ You have been unable to lose the excess weight with traditional programs involving diet, exercise, behaviour modification and medication.

Three main surgical procedures are carried out in the management of severe obesity. The first involves the placement of an adjustable band, known as a lap band, around the stomach to reduce its size. Because your stomach is smaller, you feel full despite eating less, and so lose weight. The band is placed through a small hole in your abdomen, which is a much less invasive procedure than the two alternatives (gastric bypass or gastric sleeve surgery). To adjust the band, saline solution can be added to or removed from a small reservoir under the skin, which causes the band to expand or deflate, altering the size of your stomach and, therefore, the amount of food that can be consumed. In the early days, a small amount of fluid is placed in the band, but as the weight loss slows over time the band can be tightened.

Studies have shown that by the end of the first year, people who had undergone lap band surgery had lost half of their excess weight. After two years, the average BMI had come down from 45 to 31, with a weight loss of nearly 60 per cent of the excess weight. Noticeable improvements have been seen in people with type 2 diabetes, hypertension and high cholesterol.

Some of the problems that may occur when a lap band is in place include

✔ Prolapse of the stomach through the band, which requires replacement of the band.

✔ Rupture of the reservoir tubing, which requires a minor procedure to repair.

✔ Erosion of the band into the stomach wall, which has occurred in a small number of cases and requires replacement of the band.

✔ Gallstones, which haven't caused symptoms previously, can become more active.

The second surgical procedure is the gastric bypass operation, where the stomach is stapled to create a small pouch. A section of the small intestine is attached to the pouch so food passes through very little of the small intestine, reducing kilojoule and nutrient absorption. Because the pouch is small, you tend to eat less. Because much of the digestive system is bypassed, you also absorb fewer kilojoules. Not only is a good quality multivitamin required for life, but you also need to take supplements of calcium and iron. The usual loss of weight is two-thirds of the excess in two years.

Some of the problems of gastric bypass include

✔ The pouch may stretch.

✔ The staple line can break down.

✔ Malabsorption of iron and calcium may occur.

✔ Anaemia may occur from lack of vitamin B12.

✔ The *dumping syndrome* may occur. In this condition, stomach contents move too fast into the small intestine, provoking a lot of insulin with resultant hypoglycaemia.

The third surgical procedure is known as the *gastric sleeve*. This procedure is similar to the gastric bypass; however, the shape of the remaining stomach is slightly larger and more elongated. In this procedure, the early part of the small intestine is bypassed, causing your body to forgo absorption of some fats, vitamins and minerals. As with a gastric bypass, a good quality multivitamin is required for life. Similar problems to those that can occur with a gastric bypass (included in the preceding list) also can occur with gastric sleeves.

Both the gastric bypass and the gastric sleeve are operations that aren't easily reversible and both can have a serious impact on your health and lifestyle. Make sure you talk with your GP and diabetes care team and consider all your options before deciding on surgery.

When you have a surgical procedure as treatment for obesity, you must be willing to commit to lifelong medical and dietetic follow-up. You must undertake a program of diet and exercise, and change your behaviour towards food. You must also be determined to keep the weight off. Without these changes, the success of these procedures can be limited. These surgical procedures aren't available on Medicare at the time of writing, but may be covered by your private health fund.

If you wish to undergo any of the procedures covered in this section, discuss it with your GP and be referred to an experienced practitioner who works within a multidisciplinary health team to ensure the best success possible.

Modifying behaviour

Diet and exercise must be accompanied by changes in behaviour with respect to food. Adjusting eating behaviour makes the diet easier to stick to; some of the best techniques include the following:

- ✔ At the supermarket, buy from a list, carry only enough money for the food on that list (and no cards), and avoid aisles containing high-kilojoule treat foods such as lollies.

- ✔ Don't conscientiously clean your plate.

- ✔ Eat according to a schedule to avoid eating between meals.

- ✔ Eat all your meals at the table.

- ✔ Plate food in the kitchen.

- ✔ Set realistic goals for weight loss.

- ✔ Slow down the rate at which you eat and make the meal last.

- ✔ Turn off the TV.

- ✔ When eating out, be careful of salad dressing, alcohol and bread.

You can incorporate one technique into your life each week (or whatever period it takes) until you feel you have mastered it and have added it to your eating style. Then go on and adopt another technique.

Substituting sweeteners (kilojoule-containing and artificial)

A vast effort has been made to produce a compound that could add the pleasure of sweetness without the liabilities of sugar. If you can reduce your kilojoule intake or your glucose response by using a sweetener, an advantage does exist. Sweeteners are divided into those that contain kilojoules and those that do not. Among the kilojoule-containing sweeteners are

- **Fructose, found in fruits and berries:** Fructose is actually sweeter than table sugar (sucrose). The sweetener is absorbed more slowly from the intestine than glucose, so it raises the blood glucose more slowly.

- **Sorbitol and mannitol, sugar alcohols occurring in plants:** Sorbitol and mannitol are half as sweet as table sugar and still have some effect on blood glucose.

- **Xylitol, found in strawberries and raspberries:** Xylitol is very similar to fructose in terms of sweetness. Slowly taken up from the intestine so that it causes little change in blood glucose, xylitol doesn't cause tooth decay as often as the other nutritive sweeteners.

For people with type 2 diabetes, avoiding the sweeteners included in the preceding list is best because of their high energy intake.

The non-nutritive or artificial sweeteners are often much sweeter than table sugar. Therefore, much less of them is required to achieve the same level of sweetness as sugar. They contain minimal kilojoules and so are the sweeteners of choice. The artificial sweeteners available at the time of writing include

- **Aspartame (Hermasetas Gold and Equal):** This sweetener is more expensive than saccharin, but people seem to prefer its taste. Aspartame is 150 to 200 times sweeter than sucrose.

- **Cyclamate:** Cyclamate isn't used as a table sweetener, and can be found in some drinks, such as diet cordial, mixed with saccharin. Cyclamate is 30 times as sweet as sucrose.

- ✔ **Saccharin (Sugarella and Sugarine):** Saccharin is 300 to 400 times sweeter than sucrose, and is rapidly excreted unchanged in the urine.

- ✔ **Sucralose (Splenda):** The sweetener sucralose is 600 times sweeter than sucrose. It's available in tablets and powder form and is found in some diet drinks and diet yoghurts.

- ✔ **Stevia (PureVia):** Although it has been available overseas for many years, stevia is the newest non-nutritive sweetener on the market in Australia. It's made from a plant of South American origin and is up to 300 times sweeter than sucrose. It's available for use as a table sweetener.

Other artificial sweeteners approved for use in Australia include acesulphame-K, alitame and thaumatin. These are usually mixed with the other sweeteners and are in few Australian foods.

Kilojoule-containing (or nutritive) sweeteners are best avoided — the non-nutritive or artificial sweeteners provide the sweet taste but almost none of the extra energy that you don't need when trying to lose weight. Also, non-nutritive sweeteners won't raise your blood glucose levels like kilojoule-containing sweeteners will!

Useful foods and drinks containing artificial sweeteners are 'Diet' or 'Zero' soft drinks, low-joule jellies and cordials, reduced-sugar yoghurt and 'sugar-free' sweets such as lollies and chewing gum.

If you wish to replace sugar in recipes requiring heating (such as baking or boiling), the best substitutes are sucralose and stevia. These artificial sweeteners remain stable during cooking and most often give you the best texture and taste. However, replacing all the sugar in a recipe with either of these sweeteners doesn't always result in the same look or texture you may be used to. If this is the case, try replacing half or two-thirds of the sugar with the artificial sweetener, for a dish that both tastes and 'feels' good!

As yet, no sugar-free chocolate is available in Australia — enjoy a small serve of the real thing instead!

Reading and interpreting food labels

Most food products in Australia have a nutrition information panel (NIP). The NIP allows you to compare information to determine healthier products. You can use the panels to compare the fat, saturated fat, fibre and sodium levels of similar products.

To compare products effectively, look at the amounts in the 100-gram column, rather than the serving-size column. That way, you're comparing like with like.

As a rough guide, aim for:

- ✔ Total fat less than 10 grams per 100 grams; for milk and yoghurt, aim for less than 2 grams of fat per 100 grams.

- ✔ Saturated fat as low as possible; ideally, saturated fat should be less than 3 grams per 100 grams.

- ✔ Products with the highest fibre; look for cereals greater than 6 grams of fibre per 100 grams and bread greater than 5 grams of fibre per 100 grams.

- ✔ Cereals with less than 400 milligrams of sodium per 100 grams and bread with less than 450 milligrams per 100 grams. A low-sodium product contains less than 120 milligrams of sodium per 100 grams.

Figure 8-1 shows an example of a NIP, with the areas you should pay most attention to shaded in grey.

Nutrition Information
Servings per package: 18
Serving size: 33 grams (2 biscuits)

	Per Serving	Per 100 Grams
Energy (kJ)	492 kJ	1490 kJ
Calories (Cal)	118 Cal	356 Cal
Protein (g)	4.1 g	12.4 g
Fat — Total (g)	0.5 g	1.4 g
— Saturated fat (g)	0.1 g	0.3 g
Carbohydrate — Total (g)	22.1 g	67 g
— Sugars (g)	1.1 g	3.3 g
Dietary fibre (g)	3.6 g	11.0 g
Sodium (mg)	96 mg	290 mg

Figure 8-1: Example food label.

Chapter 9

Keeping It Moving: Exercise Plan

. . . .

In This Chapter

▶ Understanding the importance of exercise

▶ Starting an exercise program — and sticking with it

▶ Burning off that excess weight

▶ Finding the right activity for you

▶ Using weight training to improve your fitness

. . . .

*M*ore than 60 years ago, the great leaders in diabetes care declared that proper management has three major aspects:

   ✔ Appropriate medication

   ✔ Proper diet

   ✔ Sufficient exercise

Although exercise was recognised as a key element in the management triad, many people with diabetes remain inactive. We include this chapter in the hope you won't make the same mistake, and cover just how you can incorporate exercise into your daily life.

With sufficient exercise and diet, some people with type 2 diabetes can revert to a non-diabetic state. This doesn't mean that they no longer have diabetes, but it certainly means that they may not develop the long-term complications that can make life so miserable later on (refer to Chapter 5).

Why Exercise Is Important

Regular physical activity has been shown to improve overall health outcomes for people with and without diabetes alike. However, studies have shown that, for people with diabetes, exercise combined with diet and medication improves blood glucose control as well as helps delay macrovascular complications.

Macrovascular disease is prevented in the following ways by exercise, which

- Helps with weight loss in type 2 diabetes
- Lowers cholesterol and triglycerides
- Lowers blood pressure
- Lowers stress levels
- Reduces the need for insulin or drugs

Many other studies have shown that exercise helps to normalise blood glucose and reduce haemoglobin A1c in type 2 diabetes. Other benefits include improving muscle strength, increasing bone density and making you feel great!

Getting Started: Exercising When You Have Diabetes

Prior to starting a new exercise program, a person with diabetes who hasn't exercised previously should check with a doctor, especially if over the age of 35 or if diabetes has been present for ten years or longer.

You should check with your GP if you have any of the following risk factors (so that you can choose the appropriate exercise):

- A history of coronary artery disease or elevated blood pressure
- A physical limitation
- Obesity

✔ The presence of any diabetic complications like retinopathy, kidney disease or neuropathy (refer to Chapter 5)

✔ Use of medications

Once exercise is begun, the person with diabetes can do a lot to make it safe and successful. Some important steps to take include

✔ Carrying treatment for hypoglycaemia (if required)

✔ Choosing cotton socks that sit loosely around your legs or ankles, and comfortable, well-fitting shoes suitable for the type of activity

✔ Drinking plenty of water

✔ Exercising with a friend who knows the signs of hypoglycaemia and how to treat it

✔ Not exercising if your blood glucose is greater than 15 mmol/L or if you're feeling unwell

✔ Testing the blood glucose more often to understand what happens when you exercise

✔ Thinking about the timing, intensity and duration of the exercise

✔ Understanding insulin action (if on insulin) and when it's working at its peak

✔ Wearing a medical alert bracelet

If you have diabetes, when exercising, you don't need to

✔ Buy special clothing other than the right shoes and socks (and possibly cycle shorts if you're bike riding)

✔ Expect to lose weight from certain 'spots' by repetitively exercising them

✔ Exercise to the point of pain

✔ Use exercise gadgets like belts or other objects that don't require you to move

Don't continue exercising if you have tightness in your chest, chest pain, severe shortness of breath or dizziness. If you experience any of these symptoms, immediately see your GP or go to the emergency department of your local hospital.

Jumping online

The following sites provide information about how to exercise safely with
diabetes:

✔ **Exercise and Sports Science
Australia:** This is the professional
body representing exercise physi-
ologists. www.essa.org.au

✔ **Fitness 2 Live:** Aimed mostly at the
corporate market, this site also

has advice for individuals in both
diet and exercise. www.fitness
2live.com.au

✔ **University of NSW Lifestyle and
Strength Clinic:** This site provides information on lifestyle and
physical activity services. www.
lifestyleclinic.net.au

Getting Your Heart Pumping

To make the most of your exercise, it's important to get your
heart pumping at a faster rate, and keep it at that faster rate
for a sustained period. Just walking sedately around a shopping
centre isn't going to make things happen!

Aerobic exercise is exercise that requires oxygen and can be
sustained for more than a few minutes, uses major groups of
muscles and gets your heart to pump faster during the exercise.
We give you many examples of aerobic exercise throughout
this chapter. *Anaerobic exercise*, on the other hand, doesn't use
oxygen and is brief (sometimes a few seconds) and intense, and
usually can't be sustained. Lifting weights or a 100-metre sprint
are examples of anaerobic exercise.

To get the most from the activity that you do and start to burn
fat, you should try to do exercise that's aerobically based and
requires some effort. The number of kilojoules you use for any
exercise is determined by your weight, the intensity of the
activity and the time you spend doing it. In order to have a
positive effect on your heart, you need to do a moderate level of
exercise for 30 to 45 minutes at least three times per week.

Moderate exercise is a moving definition. If you're out of shape,
then moderate exercise may be slow walking. On the other hand,
if you're in good shape, moderate exercise may be jogging or
hiking. Moderate exercise is simply something you can do and
not get out of breath.

You want to exercise to a level of 'somewhat hard' — about to the point where you're breathing more heavily but can still talk. As you get into shape, the amount of exertion that corresponds to 'somewhat hard' increases, meaning you need to increase the intensity or duration of your exercise to keep getting the benefits of the exercise.

Although you only need to do aerobic exercise three or four times per week to have an effect on your heart fitness, a daily program of aerobic exercise has a major impact on your diabetes. Undertaking moderate aerobic exercise for 30 to 45 minutes every day provides enormous physical, mental and emotional benefits. The choices of activities are really limitless (see the section 'Is Golf a Sport? Choosing Your Activity' later in this chapter for more on this).

You should exercise whenever you will do it faithfully. If you like to sleep late but schedule your exercise for 5.30 am, you probably won't consistently exercise, so pick a time that works in with your energy levels. Also bear in mind your eating habits. Your best time to exercise is probably about 60 to 90 minutes after eating because this is when the glucose is peaking, providing the kilojoules you need. Exercising around this period means you avoid the usual post-eating high in your blood glucose and burn up those food kilojoules. You also need to warm up and cool down for about five minutes before and after you exercise.

Even if on holidays, try to keep your regular activity going! After only about two to three weeks you start to lose some of the fitness your exercise has provided. Then getting back to your current level can take up to six weeks, assuming that your holiday from exercise doesn't go on too long.

Is Golf a Sport? Choosing Your Activity

While all physical activity is beneficial, you should choose an activity that best meets your goals and is safe for you. The following factors can help you to determine your choice of activity:

- ✔ Do you like to exercise alone or with company? Pick a competitive or team sport if you prefer company.

✔ Do you like to compete against others or just yourself? Running or walking are sports you can do alone.

✔ Do you prefer vigorous or less vigorous activity? Less vigorous activity over a longer period is just as effective as more vigorous activity undertaken for shorter periods.

✔ Do you live where you can do activities outside all year, or do you need to be inside a lot of the year? Find a sports club, gym or fitness centre if weather prevents year-round outdoor activity.

✔ Do you need special equipment or just a pair of running shoes? Special equipment is very helpful when it's needed.

✔ What benefits are you looking for in your exercise: Cardiovascular, strength, endurance, flexibility or body fat control? You should probably look for all these benefits, but you may have to combine activities to get them all in.

Perhaps a good starting point in your activity selection is to focus on the benefits. Table 9-1 gives you some ideas.

Table 9-1	Match Your Activity to the Results You Want
If You Want to ...	*Then Consider ...*
Build up cardiovascular condition	Vigorous basketball or netball, squash, hiking, brisk walking, running, dancing, cycling, boxing, soccer
Strengthen your body	Low-size, high-repetition weight-lifting, gymnastics, rock climbing, hiking, brisk walking, yoga
Build up muscular endurance	Rowing, hiking, brisk walking, vigorous basketball or netball, swimming, cycling, boxing
Increase flexibility	Gymnastics, yoga, tae-kwon-do and kick boxing, soccer, surfing, football, Pilates
Control body fat	Squash, singles tennis, hiking, brisk walking, running, dancing, vigorous basketball or netball, walking, cycling

You can tell from Table 9-1 that living in a rural setting where you have plenty of interesting scenery and terrain is helpful because hiking and walking are in practically every list. On the other hand, walking your local streets can be just as enjoyable (and social) and many urban areas now have walking and cycling tracks. You can also use the walking and cycling machines in your local gym, so you don't have to give up exercise if you live in the city.

Picking an activity that suits you over the long term

The special needs of many sports (refer to Table 9-1) may turn you off exercising. The curious thing is that the best exercise that you can sustain for life is right at your feet. A brisk daily walk improves heart function, adds to muscular endurance and helps control body fat.

Of course, the social benefits of exercise are very important. You are together with people who are concerned with health and wellbeing. These people usually share many of your interests — for example, the person who likes to jog often likes to hike and climb and go camping. Many lifetime partnerships begin on one side of a tennis court (and some end there as well).

Cross-training, where you do several different activities throughout the week, is a good idea. Cross-training reduces the boredom that may accompany one thing done day after day. It also permits you to exercise regardless of the weather because you can do some things indoors and some outside.

Everything you do burns kilojoules — even sleeping and watching television. But the more you do, and the longer you do it, the more kilojoules you burn.

Taking your current physical condition into account

Your choice of an activity must take into account your physical condition. Certain activities aren't suitable for people with certain conditions, especially some of the long-term complications of diabetes (refer to Chapter 5 for more).

If you have diabetic neuropathy and can't feel your feet, you shouldn't do pounding exercises that may damage your feet without your awareness. You can, however, swim, cycle, row or do armchair exercises where you move your upper body vigorously.

If you have diabetic retinopathy, you shouldn't do exercises that raise your blood pressure (like weight-lifting), cause jerky motions in your eyes (like bouncing on a trampoline), or change the pressure in your eyes significantly (like scuba diving or high mountain climbing). You also shouldn't do exercises that involve lowering your eyes below the level of your heart, such as when you touch your toes.

If you have kidney disease, you should avoid exercises that raise your blood pressure for prolonged periods. These exercises are extremely intense activities that you do for a long time, like marathon running.

Some people have pain in their legs after they walk a certain distance. This may be due to diminished blood supply to the legs, meaning the needs of the muscles in the legs aren't met by the inadequate blood supply. Although you need to discuss this problem with your doctor, you don't need to give up walking. Determine the distance you can walk up to the point of pain. Walk about three-quarters of that distance and then stop to give the circulation a chance to catch up. Once you have rested, you can go about the same distance again without pain. By stringing several of these walks together, you can get a good, pain-free workout. You may even find that you're able to increase the distance after a while because this kind of training tends to create new blood vessels.

Short of chest pain at rest, which must be addressed by your doctor, no medical condition should prevent you from doing any sort of exercise at all. If you can't work out an exercise that you can do, get together with an exercise physiologist or your local gym instructor. You may be amazed at how many muscles you can move that you never knew you had.

Lifting Weights and Getting Fit

Weight-lifting is a form of anaerobic exercise (refer to the section 'Getting Your Heart Pumping' earlier in this chapter if you're not sure what this is). It involves the movement of heavy weights, which can only be moved for brief periods of time. It results in significant muscle strengthening and increased endurance.

Because weight-lifting causes a significant rise in blood pressure as it's being done, people with severe diabetic eye disease shouldn't do it.

Strength training, which uses lighter weights, can be a form of aerobic exercise. Because the weights are light, they can be moved for prolonged periods of time. The result is improved cardiovascular fitness along with strengthening of muscles, tendons, ligaments and bones. Strength training is an excellent way to protect and strengthen a joint that's beginning to develop some discomfort.

Strength training may be good for the days that you don't do your other aerobic exercise, such as walking or cycling, or you can add it for a few minutes after you finish your activity. Strength training is also good for working on a particular group of muscles that you feel is weak. Very often, this muscle is the back. Strength-training exercises can isolate and strengthen each muscle. If you do a lot of aerobic exercise that involves the legs, you may want to use upper-body strength training only.

Part IV
The Part of Tens

Glenn Lumsden

'The doctor told me it was crucial that I receive hour-long foot massages every day.'

In this part ...

*I*n this part, you get key techniques for preventing or reversing the effects of diabetes. You also get ten major myths about diabetes that you can discard. With just a little background from the other parts in this book, you can use these two chapters to really finetune your diabetes care.

Chapter 10

Ten Ways to Prevent or Reverse Diabetes

. . . .

In This Chapter

▶ Manoeuvring major health monitoring

▶ Coming around to considered consumption

▶ Tackling tenacious testing

▶ Executing enthusiastic exercising

▶ Looking at lifelong learning

▶ Medicating meticulously

▶ Adopting an appropriate attitude

▶ Planning preventive processes

▶ Embracing fastidious footcare and essential eyecare

. . . .

*I*f you've read everything that came before this chapter, congratulations. But we didn't expect you to (and besides, this is a reference book, not a novel) and that's why we wrote this chapter. Follow our advice in this chapter, and you can be in great shape with your diabetes.

Monitoring Your Blood Glucose

You have your glucose meter. Now what do you do with it? Most people don't like to prick themselves and are reluctant to do so at first. How often you test is between you and your doctor, but the more you do it, the easier it is to control your diabetes. Monitoring gives you more insight into your particular response to food, exercise and medications. (Refer to Chapter 6 for more on monitoring blood glucose.)

People who have stable type 2 diabetes may test once per day at different times or more often if medication is changing or if readings seem higher than usual.

Always take your blood glucose readings along when visiting your GP or any of the members of your diabetes care team — If you give a lot of information, people can be more specific with the advice and assistance they provide.

If you're sick or about to start a long drive, you might want to test more often because you don't want to become hypo-glycaemic — or hyperglycaemic for that matter. The beauty of the meter is that you can check your blood glucose in less than 30 seconds any time you feel it's necessary.

Being Careful with What You Eat

If you are what you eat, you have a pretty good incentive to consider your consumption carefully. If you gain weight, you gain insulin resistance, but it doesn't take a lot of weight loss to reverse the situation. The main point you should understand about a diet for diabetes is that it's a healthy diet for anyone, whether they have diabetes or not. You shouldn't feel like a social outcast because you're eating the right foods. You don't need special supplements; the diet is balanced and contains all the vitamins and minerals you require (although you want to be sure you're getting enough calcium).

You can follow a diet for diabetes wherever you are, not just at home. Every menu has something on it that's appropriate for you. If you're invited to someone's home, tell your host you have diabetes and to be unconcerned if you don't accept the offer of seconds or a large portion of dessert!

Having Tests Regularly

The companies who make smoke detectors recommend that you change the battery without fail each time the clocks go back at the end of daylight saving. (If you live in a state or territory without daylight saving, you need to use another regular event, such as your birthday.)

We recommend that you use this simple annual reminder to get your 'complication detectors' checked. Make sure that your doctor checks your urine for tiny amounts of protein and your feet for loss of sensation every year. Once you know the problem is present, you can do a lot to slow it down or even reverse it. Never has it been more true that 'an ounce of prevention is worth a pound of cure'. (For more on complications you may develop, refer to Chapters 4 and 5.)

Keeping Active

Keeping active can help your diabetes in many different ways. It can help your muscles become more sensitive to insulin, it may help you lose weight and it can reduce your risk of heart disease. Exercise can be used to burn up glucose in place of insulin, thereby lowering your blood glucose even without losing weight. We're not talking about an hour of running or 100 kilometres on the bike; moderate exercise like brisk walking can accomplish the same thing. The key is to exercise regularly. (For more on exercise, refer to Chapter 9.)

Educating Yourself

So much is going on in the field of diabetes that even we have trouble keeping up with it, and it's our speciality! How can you expect to know when the doctors come up with the major advances that will cure your diabetes? The answer is lifelong learning.

Once you have got past the shock of the diagnosis, you're ready to learn. This book contains a lot of basic information that you need to know. You can even take a course in diabetes self-management. These are often provided by local diabetes care teams or in community health centres. The Australian Diabetes Council (in NSW) or Diabetes Australia (in other states and territories) also run courses and can help you find the closest ones to you.

Then you need to keep learning. Become a member of Diabetes Australia and get access to the terrific magazine called *Conquest*, which usually contains information on the latest in diabetes management. In some states, the publication may not be directly posted to you, but if you go to the Diabetes Australia website (www.diabetesaustralia.com.au) you can access past copies online. Diabetes Australia is also working with Pacific Magazines to provide editorial review of their magazine *Diabetic Living*, which is available in newsagencies and supermarkets.

Heeding the Doctor's Advice

Treating your disease in accordance with your doctor's instructions is always beneficial. Certainly, taking medication can be a pain (even if you could take insulin by mouth and not by injection). The basic assumption in diabetes care is that you're taking your medication regularly — your doctor bases all his or her decisions on that assumption. Some very serious mistakes can be made if that assumption is false. Diabetes medications are pretty potent, and too much of a good thing can be bad for you. (For more on medications, refer to Chapter 7.)

Every time a study is done on why people with diabetes don't do better, the lack of regularity in taking medications is high up or leads the list of reasons. Do you make a conscious decision to miss your tablets, or do you forget? Perhaps just not enough money is left at the end of the month for the script to be filled. Whatever the reason, the best thing to do is to set up a system that works for you. Keeping your tablets in a dated container quickly shows you if you have taken them or not. You might even divide the tablets by time of day. Make the system simple so that it works for you. Speak with your diabetes care team if finances are a problem — they may be able to help.

Maintaining a Positive Outlook

Your approach to your condition can go a long way towards determining whether you live in diabetes heaven or diabetes hell. It can help to see your diabetes as a challenge and an opportunity.

Diabetes is a challenge because you have to think about doing certain things that others never have to worry about. It brings out the quality of organisation, which can then be transferred to other parts of your life.

Diabetes is an opportunity because it encourages you to make healthy choices for your diet as well as your exercise. You may well end up a lot healthier than your neighbour without diabetes. As you make more and more healthy choices, you feel and test less and less like a person with diabetes. Does this mean that at some point you can give up your treatment? Probably not, although you'll most likely be able to take less medication — and feel a lot better!

Being Prepared

Life is full of surprises. You never know when you're going to get more than you bargained for. That's why having a plan to deal with the unexpected is useful.

There is great stress at work or at home. Does this throw you off your diet, your exercise and taking your medications? You go off travelling and get food poisoning or an upset stomach. Are you prepared and do you know what to do?

 You might even do a 'dry run'. Go to the website of a restaurant that you might like to try and read their menu. Think about and select the foods that can help you to stay in control. If you have questions, ask your diabetes care team. Practising handling these situations before they arise makes it a lot easier to function when you're faced with the real thing.

Examining Your Feet

A recent headline read: 'Hospital sued by seven foot doctors'. We would certainly not like to treat any doctor with seven feet or even a doctor who is seven feet tall. Whether you have two feet or seven feet, you must take good care of them.

Although diabetes is a major source of foot amputations, these kinds of operations are entirely preventable — but you must pay attention to your feet. Problems occur when you can't feel with your feet because of neuropathy (refer to Chapter 5). You can easily find out when this is present by getting your GP to check with a monofilament. If your feet can't feel the filament, they may not feel burning hot water, a stone or nail in your shoe or an infected ulcer on your foot.

Once you lose sensation in your feet, your eyes must replace the pain fibres that would otherwise tell you a problem is developing. You need to examine your feet carefully every day, keep your toenails trimmed and wear comfortable shoes. Your GP should be inspecting your feet at every visit. Test bath water by hand, shake your shoes out before you put them on and wear new shoes only for a short while before checking for pressure spots. The future of your feet is in your hands. (For more on caring for your feet, refer to Chapter 5.)

Focusing On Your Eyes

You're reading this book, which means you're seeing this book. So far, no plans are being developed to put out a braille edition, so you better take care of your eyes or you will miss out on the wonderful gems of information that brighten every page.

Eyecare starts with a careful examination by an optometrist or ophthalmologist. You need to have an exam at least once per year (or more often if necessary). If your diabetes is well controlled, the doctor finds two normal eyes. If not, signs of diabetic eye disease may show up (refer to Chapter 5). At that point, you need to control your diabetes, which means controlling your blood glucose. You also want to control your blood pressure because high blood pressure contributes to worsening eye disease.

Although the final word is not in on the effects of smoking and excessive alcohol on eye disease in diabetes, is it worth risking your sight for another puff of a cigarette? Even at this late stage, you can stop the progression of the eye disease or reverse some of the damage.

Chapter 11

Ten Myths about Diabetes That You Can Forget

*M*yths are a lot of fun. They're never completely true, but you can usually find a tiny bit of truth in a myth — which is one reason (along with the need for an explanation when 'science' fails to provide one) so many myths are believed.

The trouble is that some myths can harm you if you allow them to determine your medical care. This chapter is about those kinds of myths — the ones that lead you to not take your medication or eat a well-balanced diet or even to take things that may not be good for you. The ten myths in this chapter are only a small sample of all the myths that exist about diabetes. They could take up a whole book on their own. But the myths we describe here are some of the more important ones. Realising that these are myths can help prevent you from making some serious mistakes about good diabetes care.

Following Treatment Perfectly Yields Perfect Glucose Levels

Doctors are probably as responsible as their patients are for the myth that perfect treatment results in perfect glucoses. For decades, doctors measured the urine glucose and told their patients that if they would just stay on their diet, take their medication and get their exercise, the urine would be negative for glucose.

Doctors failed to account for the many variables that could result in a positive test for glucose in the urine, plus the fact that even if the urine was negative, the patient could still be experiencing diabetic damage (because the urine becomes negative at a blood glucose of around 10 mmol/L in most people, a level that still causes damage).

The same thing is true for the blood glucose. Although you can achieve normal blood glucose levels most of the time if you treat your diabetes properly, you can still have times when, for no apparent reason, the glucose isn't normal. When you consider that so many factors can determine the blood glucose level at any given time, this variation should hardly be a surprise. These factors include

✔ Your diet

✔ Your exercise

✔ Your medication

✔ Your emotional state

✔ Other illnesses

✔ The day of your menstrual cycle (if a woman)

The miracle is that the blood glucose is what you expect it to be as often as it is. Don't allow an occasional unexpected result to throw you. Keep on doing what you know to be right, and your overall control will be excellent.

Eating a Slice of Cake Can Kill You

Some people can become fanatical when they develop diabetes. They think that they must be perfect in every aspect of their diabetes care and can drive themselves crazy with their belief that they must follow the 'perfect diet' all the time.

Now, doctors may be at fault here, having told their patients that they must avoid sugar at all costs! As Chapter 8 shows, doctors and your diabetes care team now understand that a little sugar in the diet isn't harmful. They also appreciate that some regular 'treat' foods can be helpful in keeping you motivated to keep eating well for the majority of the time.

This myth goes back again to the fact that science doesn't have all the answers. Knowledge is still evolving. It may never reach the point where the statement made to Woody Allen's character in the movie *Sleeper* is true. He wakes up after sleeping for 100 years and is told that scientists now realise that milkshakes and fatty meats are good for you. But who knows?

The bottom line is occasional dietary lapses aren't harmful. No-one is perfect — not even your diabetes care team, and not even you! Don't feel the need to have a perfect diet all the time.

You Can Tell the Level of Your Blood Glucose by How You Feel

Actually, this is a very common myth that people tell us all the time. To look at this scientifically, a research study was conducted whereby people with diabetes were hooked up to glucose and insulin intravenous lines so researchers could manipulate their blood glucose levels.

Participants were 'given' a particular blood glucose level and asked to say what it was. The number of correct answers was pretty bad — most people couldn't even accurately tell if they were hypoglycaemic (blood glucose too low) or hyperglycaemic (blood glucose too high)!

The moral of the story: Test your blood glucose at your required intervals, and especially if you think you are high or low. Guessing may lead you in exactly the wrong direction with your treatment, which causes more problems.

Finding a Cure in Unorthodox Methods

Many health or weight-loss treatments don't help you and may harm you. Whenever a problem affects a huge number of people, others are eager to exploit this potential goldmine.

How can you know if what you read in your favourite magazine or see on the internet is actually useful? Check it out with your GP, your diabetes educator or other members of your diabetes care team. They will know or can find out for you about any appropriate treatment. To date, diabetes has no simple cures. A book or organisation that promises an easy cure isn't doing you any favours.

Diabetes Ends Spontaneity

You may think that your freedom to eat when you want and come and go as you please is gone once you have diabetes. This myth is far from the truth.

Do you have to give up eating out if you have diabetes? Of course not — it's one of life's great pleasures! Newer oral agents for type 2 diabetes allow you to eat when you want and anticipate that the blood glucose levels are going to remain within or close to target range.

Should you dance the night away even though you have diabetes? Of course you should! Oral medications are unlikely to need adjustment for these occasional situations.

Can you travel where you want with diabetes? Most certainly. You just need to plan your trip in advance so you can get together all the bits and pieces you need in time. For example, make sure that you have a list of your medications with you to show customs if requested. Keep your medications with you so that if your luggage gets lost, your medicine doesn't go with it. Purchase travel insurance — even if it's a bit more expensive because of your diabetes, it's invaluable if you have the misfortune of something going wrong while you're overseas. These three things are now simple to do and can ensure that diabetes doesn't affect your trip.

Needing Insulin Means You're Doomed

Many people with type 2 diabetes believe that once they have to take insulin, they're on a rapid downhill course to death. This is not true. Once you're using insulin, it probably means that your pancreas has conked out and can't produce enough insulin to control your blood glucose, even when stimulated by oral drugs. But taking insulin is no more a death sentence for you than it is for the person with type 1 diabetes.

Sometimes using insulin is a temporary measure for when you're very sick with some other illness that makes your oral drugs ineffective. Once the illness is over, your need for insulin ends. Other times, insulin is commenced because the oral medications you're using can no longer keep your blood glucose levels in the target range and using insulin is your only alternative to keep you well.

The majority of people with type 2 diabetes eventually end up needing insulin injections. If the recent jump in the number of new medications used to manage diabetes is any indication of things to come, this may soon become a thing of the past; however, for now, if you do require insulin try not to be afraid or anxious about it. Your diabetes care team are there to help you cope with a new way to manage your diabetes and can make the process as easy for you as possible.

Occasionally people with diabetes who have been on insulin for some time after 'failing' oral agents can be taken off the insulin and given one of the newer oral agents, which actually controls their glucose better than the insulin. One typical patient was on 40 units of insulin weighing 82 kilograms with an HbA1c of 7.4 per cent. His insulin dose was gradually lowered as Byetta (refer to Chapter 7) was added to his treatment. He lost 5 kilograms, came off insulin entirely and now has a HbA1c of 6.5 per cent.

Older people with diabetes may need insulin to keep their blood glucose at a reasonable level but don't need very tight control because their probable life span is shorter than the time it takes to develop complications. Their treatment can be kept very simple. The insulin is being used to keep them 'out of trouble', not to prevent long-term complications.

Finally, people with type 2 diabetes who truly need to be on insulin often find once they have taken the plunge to start insulin that they feel much better and making the change was actually a good thing.

People with Diabetes Shouldn't Exercise

If any myth is really damaging to people with diabetes, it is this one: People with diabetes shouldn't exercise. The truth is exactly the opposite. Exercise is a major component of good diabetes management, one that, unfortunately, all too often gets the least time and effort on the part of the person with diabetes as well as care providers.

Of course, if you have certain complications like haemorrhaging in your eye or severe neuropathy, you need to take precautions or not exercise at all for a time. Certainly, if you're older than 40 and haven't exercised, you need to start gradually. Except for these and a few other reasons (refer to Chapter 9), exercise ought to be done regularly by every person with diabetes.

And we're not just talking about aerobic exercise where your heart is beating faster. Some form of muscle strengthening also needs to be a part of your lifestyle. (Refer to Chapter 9 to find out the benefits of muscle strengthening.) If you have a muscle that you can move, move it!

Getting Life and Health Insurance Is Impossible

Even if you have type 2 diabetes, you *can* get life and health insurance. Because the insurance industry recognises that people with diabetes often take better care of themselves than the general population does, it is more and more willing to insure them. Some unenlightened insurance companies still exist, but most are seeing the light as the vital statistics of the population with diabetes improve. However, life and travel insurance premiums are likely to be higher if you have diabetes.

Private health insurance to supplement your Medicare-funded diabetes care may be beneficial for some people with diabetes. You may be concerned about public hospital waiting lists for procedures such as heart bypasses or knee replacements.

You may need to shop around to find the health insurance scheme that best suits your needs, but the price should be no higher than what anyone else is paying.

Most Diabetes Is Inherited

Although type 2 diabetes runs in families, the condition doesn't come out in every family member. Whether you develop type 2 diabetes or not can depend on such things as body weight, level of activity and other factors.

Parents shouldn't feel guilty or blame themselves if their child or adolescent develops diabetes. Feeling guilty only makes it harder to care for and live with your child who has diabetes. Talk to your doctor or diabetes care team about feelings of guilt, anger or frustration.

Diabetes Wrecks Your Sense of Humour

While at first you may not feel like laughing, after the initial stages of accepting diabetes your sense of humour should return. If your humour doesn't return, it's no laughing matter, so seek some expert help.

The saying goes, 'Someday, we'll laugh about this'. The question is, 'Why wait?'

Glossary

advanced glycosylation (glycated) end products (AGEs): Chemical combinations of *glucose* with other substances in the body. Too much may damage various organs.

amino acids: Compounds that link together to form proteins.

angiography: Using a dye injected into the bloodstream to take pictures of blood vessels to detect disease. In diabetes, angiography is often used in the eyes and coronary arteries.

atherosclerosis (arteriosclerosis): Narrowing of arteries due to deposits of cholesterol and other factors. Can occur in the heart (cardiovascular disease), in the brain (cerebrovascular disease) or in the legs (peripheral vascular disease).

autonomic neuropathy: Diseases of nerves that affect organs not under conscious control, such as the heart, intestine and blood vessels.

background retinopathy: An early stage of diabetic eye involvement that doesn't reduce vision.

beta cells: Cells in the Islets of Langerhans in the *pancreas*, which make the key hormone insulin.

body mass index: A number derived by dividing the weight (in kilograms) by the height times the height (in metres). Used to determine the category of weight (either underweight, normal, overweight or obese).

cataract: A clouding of the lens of the eye often found earlier and more commonly in people with diabetes.

cerebrovascular disease (CVD): A disease of the arteries that supply the brain with blood, carrying oxygen and nutrients.

cholesterol: A form of fat that's needed in the body for production of certain hormones. Can lead to *atherosclerosis* if present in excessive levels.

creatinine: A substance in blood that's measured to reflect the level of kidney function.

dialysis: Artificial filtering to clean the blood when the kidneys aren't working properly.

endocrinologist: A doctor who specialises in diseases of the hormone-producing glands, including the adrenal glands, the thyroid, the pituitary, the parathyroid glands, the ovaries, testicles and pancreas.

exercise physiologist: A health professional who specialises in the delivery of exercise, lifestyle and behavioural modification programs for the prevention and management of chronic diseases and injuries.

fibre: A substance in plants that can't be digested, so provides no energy. It can lower fat and blood glucose if it dissolves in water and is absorbed or can help prevent constipation if it doesn't dissolve in water and remains in the intestine.

glucometer: A machine designed to measure blood glucose levels.

glucose: The body's main source of energy in the blood and cells.

glycaemic index: The speed at which a given food raises blood glucose, usually compared to 50 grams of pure glucose. Low glycaemic index foods are preferred in diabetes.

glycogen: The storage form of glucose in the liver and muscles.

glycosuria: Glucose in the urine.

haemoglobin A1c: A measurement of blood glucose control reflecting the average blood glucose for the last 60 to 90 days.

high density lipoprotein (HDL) cholesterol: A particle in blood that carries cholesterol and helps reduce *atherosclerosis*.

hyperglycaemia: Elevated levels of blood glucose; greater than 7 mmol/L fasting or 7.8 mmol/L after food.

hyperglycaemic hyperosmolar state: Very high glucose in type 2 diabetes associated with severe dehydration but not excessive fat breakdown and acidosis. It can lead to coma and death. Previously known as hyperosmolar non-ketotic state (or HONK).

hyperinsulinaemia: More insulin than normal in the blood, often found early in type 2 diabetes.

hyperlipidaemia: Elevated levels of fat in the blood.

hypoglycaemia: Levels of blood glucose lower than normal, usually less than 4.0 mmol/L. Usually caused by excessive amounts of insulin and/or too much exercise and/or too little food.

impaired fasting glucose (IFG): Levels of glucose between 6.1 and 6.9 mmol/L when in a fasting state. Not normal, but not high enough to be diagnosed as diabetes.

impaired glucose tolerance (IGT): Levels of glucose between 7.8 and 11.1 mmol/L after eating. Not normal but not quite high enough for a diagnosis of diabetes.

insulin: The key hormone that controls blood *glucose*; it permits glucose to enter cells and stops the liver overproducing glucose.

insulin resistance: Decreased response to insulin found early in type 2 diabetes.

islet cells: The cells in the *pancreas* that make *insulin*, glucagon and other hormones.

lancet: A sharp needle to prick the skin for a blood glucose test.

laser treatment: Using a device that burns tiny areas in the back of the eye to prevent worsening of *retinopathy*.

low density lipoprotein (LDL): A particle in the blood containing cholesterol and thought to be responsible for *atherosclerosis*.

macrovascular complications: Heart attack, stroke or diminished blood flow to the legs.

metabolic syndrome: A combination of hypertension, increased abdominal fat, high triglycerides, low HDL cholesterol, often obesity, and high uric acid associated with diabetes and increased heart attacks.

microalbuminuria: Loss of small but abnormal amounts of protein in the urine.

microvascular complications: Eye disease, nerve disease or kidney disease.

monounsaturated fat: One form of fat from vegetable sources like olives and nuts that doesn't raise cholesterol.

National Diabetes Services Scheme (NDSS): Federal government–funded scheme administered by Diabetes Australia to subsidise the cost of diabetes supplies.

nephropathy: Damage to the kidneys.

neuropathic ulcer: An infected area usually on the leg or foot resulting from damage that wasn't felt because of *neuropathy*.

neuropathy: Damage to nerves, particularly those carrying sensation in the legs and feet.

ophthalmologist: A doctor who specialises in diseases of the eyes.

oral glucose tolerance test (OGTT): This test can determine the difference between having *prediabetes* and diabetes. It involves fasting overnight, having your blood glucose tested, then drinking a glucose-containing drink, followed by further measurements of your blood glucose levels at one hour and two hours.

oral hypoglycaemic agent: A glucose-lowering drug taken by mouth.

pancreas: The organ behind the stomach that contains the *islet cells*.

polydipsia: Excessive intake of water or other fluids.

polyunsaturated fat: A form of fat from vegetables that may not raise cholesterol but lowers *high density lipoprotein (HDL) cholesterol*.

polyuria: Excessive urination.

prediabetes: The term used to describe impaired fasting glucose or impaired glucose tolerance, often the precursors for diabetes.

proliferative retinopathy: Undesirable proliferation of blood vessels in front of the *retina*.

proteinuria: Abnormal loss of protein from the body into the urine.

retina: The part of the eye that senses light.

retinopathy: Disease of the *retina*.

very low density lipoprotein (VLDL): The main particle in the blood that carries triglycerides.

Index

FOR DUMMIES®

Health, Fitness & Pregnancy

978-0-73037-500-5
$39.95

978-0-73140-760-6
$34.95

978-1-74246-844-0
$39.95

978-0-73037-664-4
$39.95

978-0-73037-660-6
$39.95

978-0-73037-536-4
$39.95

978-1-74216-984-2
$39.95

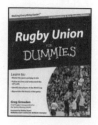

978-0-73037-656-9
$39.95

978-1-74216-946-0
$39.95

978-0-73037-739-9
$39.95

978-0-73037-735-1
$19.95

978-1-74216-972-9
$39.95

FOR DUMMIES®

Reference

978-1-74216-999-6
$39.95

978-1-74216-982-8
$39.95

978-1-74216-983-5
$45.00

978-0-73037-699-6
$39.95

Business & Investing

978-1-74216-977-4
$29.95

978-0-73037-668-2
$19.95

978-1-11822-291-1
$24.95

978-1-74216-962-0
$19.95

Technology

978-0-47049-743-2
$32.95

978-1-74246-896-9
$39.95

978-1-74216-998-9
$45.00

978-0-47048-998-7
$32.95